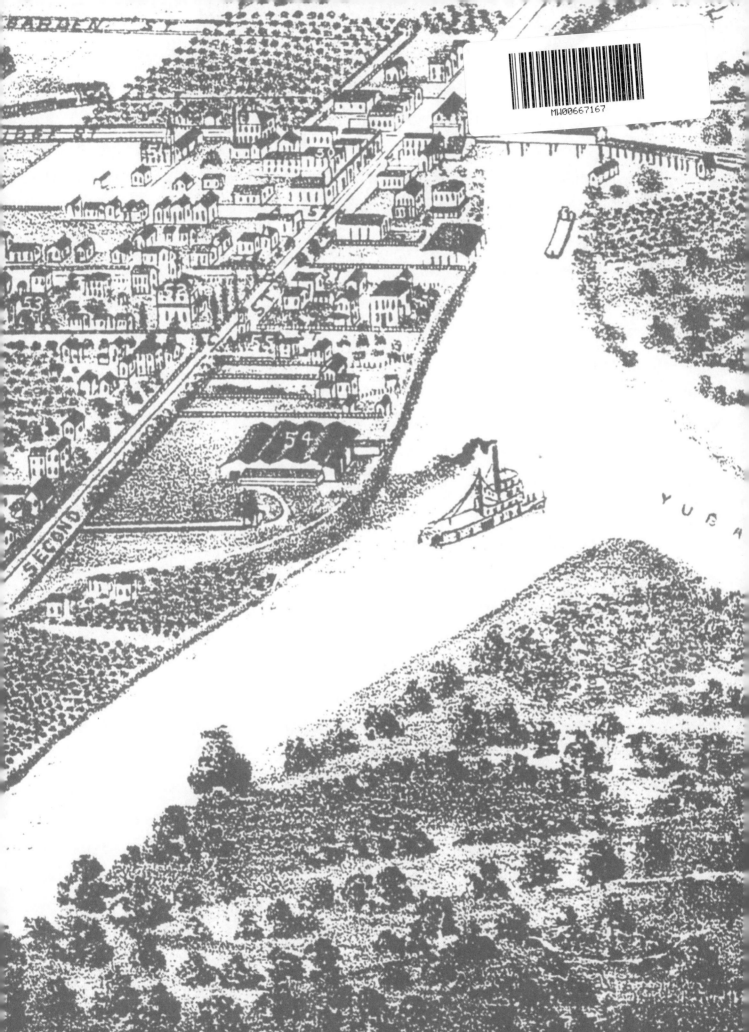

Yuba City
OUR HOME TOWN

David M. Rubiales

Carol Withington

Sharyl Simmons

Janie Stark

THE
DONNING COMPANY
PUBLISHERS

Yuba City
OUR HOME TOWN

by Julie Stark,
Sharyl Simmons,
David M. Rubiales, and
Carol Withington

The Donning Company Publishers
184 Business Park Drive, Suite 206
Virginia Beach, VA 23462

Steve Mull, General Manager
Barbara Buchanan, Office Manager
Heather Floyd, Editor
Amanda D. Guilmain, Graphic Designer
Derek Eley, Imaging Artist
Debby Dowell, Project Research Coordinator
Scott Rule, Director of Marketing
Tonya Hannink, Marketing Coordinator

Dwight Tompkins, Project Director

Library of Congress Cataloging-in-Publication Data

Yuba City, our home town / by Julie Stark ... [et al.].
    p. cm.
 Includes bibliographical references and index.
 ISBN 978-1-57864-498-8 (hardcover : alk. paper)
 1. Yuba City (Calif.)--History. 2. Yuba City (Calif.)--Social life and customs. 3. Yuba City (Calif.)--Economic conditions. 4. Yuba City (Calif.)--Pictorial works. 5. Historic sites--California--Yuba City--Pictorial works. I. Stark, Julie.
 F869.Y76Y83 2008
 979.4'34--dc22
                                              2008011460

Printed in the United States of America at Walsworth Publishing Company

On Yuba City

The Yuba City silent stands
Where Providence has placed her,
The glory passed to other hands,
That should by right have graced her.

She stands with aspect sad but high,
And gazes on the river
That like a stranger passes by
And nothing has to give her.

Alas, that beauty thus should fade
Or live so unregarded,
And all the efforts art has made
Pass fruitless, unrewarded!

Are not her groves most fair to see,
Her paths most greenly-skirted?
What has she said, or done, to be
Thus doomed and thus deserted?

[...]

I've seen her at the morning prime—
The sky looked sweeter, bluer;
I've seen her at the evening time—
The stars seemed bending to her!

Oh, Yuba City, 'tis a sin
Thou art lonely and forsaken
When uglier cities favor win
And prosperous paths have taken.

Who seek for loveliness will meet
The picture where they find thee—
The Feather River at thy feet,
The lofty Buttes behind thee;

And they will bless the quiet scene,
That holds thee like a jewel,
And weep that thou'st abandoned been
To fortunes cold and cruel.

But, Yuba City, time will cast
The changes in thy favor;
Then, in redemption of the past,
Thou'lt stand, whilst others waver.

John Rollin Ridge, Cherokee chief,
Victorian poet, and Marysville
newspaper editor, who had recently
moved from Yuba City to Marysville,
wrote and published this lament
over the nearly deserted city in the
April 29, 1851 *Marysville Herald*.

Green
Marysville

Yuba City
CONTENTS

PREFACE

This book grew out of a deep community need. The early history of Yuba City was briefly touched on in the 1879 and the 1924 county history books, but we have never had a book of our town history.

The centennial of Yuba City's incorporation afforded the opportunity to create the book our community has been seeking, so the staff of the Community Memorial Museum set about to tackle the project.

We were fortunate to gather an excellent group of volunteer writers, historians, researchers, and consultants to help in the endeavor. The museum's Assistant Curator Sharyl Simmons, a capable historian in her own right, and I served as writers and editors. Professor David Rubiales of Yuba College wrote the prehistory and generously shared it. Museum volunteer Carol Withington researched and wrote several sections. Sharon Anthony contributed invaluable research by visiting local libraries to seek and copy old newspaper articles. Eleanor Knox researched the museum's archives for material. Photographer Allan Lamb volunteered his time and talent to photograph landmarks throughout the city and improve the quality of many of the historic photographs. Local historian Don Burtis generously shared his considerable knowledge of our history. Steve Perry shared his expertise of land-use history. Joan Erfle provided Sister City information. Bill Fuller shared valuable city history. Phyllis Smith assisted with editing. Gina Crawford generously shared her graphic designs. Many residents came forward to share cherished stories, memories, and photos. The Community Memorial Museum Commission actively supported taking on such a large project. Thanks also to the three museum helpers, Joni Adams, Eleanor Knox, and Evelyn Rusch, who handled visitors and phone calls, allowing the staff to continue work on the book. Without all of these generous, supportive volunteers, the book would never have been written.

What this book is not is a comprehensive history of Yuba City, as space does not permit it. We hope that this book is a history that touches on the highlights of human experience here and gives a flavor of what life was like in our small, rural town for the first one hundred years, from 1849 to around 1950.

If you find that some history has been omitted, we hope that will be the impetus for you to bring it to the Community Memorial Museum, so that it can be included in the next book and become part of the museum's archives. If you have photos that you would allow the museum to copy, please bring those. The museum only has as much history as the community brings to it.

A word about good grammar and punctuation is in order. You may wince as you read some of the quotes and newspaper articles. I winced a lot, but I did not change the author's original words or punctuation unless it was vital to understanding the piece. Attitudes expressed and terms used in some quotes should be considered in the context of their times.

I am pleased that this book has allowed us to share with you some of the fascinating stories of our town. I hope that you will love these stories, too.

Julie Stark
Director/Curator
Community Memorial Museum
February 2008

Yuba City
THE FIRST ONES

THE NISENAN PEOPLE

The culture encountered in the mid-Valley by the Euro-Americans was at least 3,500 years old, and perhaps the oldest continuing culture in North America.

Inhabitants of the mid-Valley concentrated on a few species of plants and animals as important staples. Acorns, deer, salmon, and hard seeds were favored, but over 200 to 300 species of plants and animals were used to sustain human life. Knowledge of local ecosystems became highly refined and sophisticated. By refining the technique of acorn leaching, which makes the acorn suitable for human consumption, and combining that with the netting of salmon in extraordinary numbers, the people of this period expanded their populations to record levels. The combination was so successful that archaeologists and anthropologists have dubbed this food combination the "acorn/salmon complex." There were plenty of other sources for food, however. The Nisenan possessed all of the benefits of agriculture and a gathering existence, but without its disadvantages and the hardships usually identified with that life.

Until this historic era, the peoples of the Sacramento Valley and other Californians who relied on the acorn/salmon complex had the largest non-agricultural population in the world. S. F. Cook estimates the pre-Columbian population of the Central Valley to have been over 100,000, with three-fourths of that population residing in the Sacramento Valley.

The Sutter Buttes

The lower Feather River region and its tributaries were inhabited by the Nisenan (also known as the Southern Maidu). Life in a Nisenan village revolved around family and community, subsistence, and imagination. Their physical world was oriented north and south, following the rivers. Villages were situated on the west side of the rivers on natural berms created by repeated flooding over the millennia. On the Feather, there were approximately twenty villages from north of present-day Gridley to the plain between the mouths of the Bear and American rivers. The sizes of the villages on both rivers varied, with some consisting of only a few dozen people, while others had much larger populations.

Each family lived in its own dwelling. Houses were dome-shaped and covered with earth, tule mats, or grass. They were usually semi-subterranean (about four feet deep), which helped cool the interior in the hot summer months and warm it in the cold winter months. Their size ranged from ten to fifteen feet across. Larger villages also had dance houses, which were considerably larger than family dwellings. In each village there was a sweathouse for men. Daily sweating was not just a spiritual event but also a function of hygiene. Native Californians were highly conscious of personal cleanliness. After sweating, the men typically plunged into a river, creek, or lake. Women also bathed daily and children were bathed regularly.

Careful attention to hygiene may have been related to customs of dress among the Nisenan. The climate was moderate for most of the year and an individual required little protection against the elements. Men wore no clothing at all in mild weather, and in colder seasons, they wore at most robes of bird feathers or rabbit fur. Women went about without clothing above the waist, but wore skirts or aprons made of tule grass or shredded bark.

Each village (or sometimes a group of villages) had a "headman" who acted as the village leader. The headman was not a chief with absolute power, but relied instead on persuasion and prestige to get other villagers to conform to his wishes. His duties included settling disputes between individuals, representing his village to other villages, and hosting ceremonies. Perhaps most importantly, he supervised the accumulation and distribution of food resources. He made sure that the villagers prepared for each season, although he did not have to work himself but relied on the other villagers to supply him with food.

The core unit of village life was the married couple with children. Courtship began when a young man, a year or two beyond puberty, indicated his affection for a particular young woman, herself not likely a year past puberty, who was acceptable to his family. After the young woman accepted her suitor's overtures, he was required to send gifts to her parents. The gifts usually consisted of food but might also have been shells and beads. After the girl and her family accepted the suitor and his gifts, he moved in with her family and lived with them for six months, spending the time hunting and fishing for his wife and in-laws. About six months after their marriage, the young couple moved to the husband's village, where they most likely spent the rest of their lives. Throughout their lives, neither husband nor wife could speak directly to, or even look directly at, their parents-in-law. This was a common taboo throughout the core of California Native American cultures.

Nisenan women were responsible for gathering and preparing food as well as cooking. They possessed extensive and sophisticated knowledge of local plants, which allowed them to maximize the resources of the local environment. Each community made sure that they stored enough acorns to last for at least a two-year period. The acorns were stored in elevated granaries that measured up to three feet in diameter and eight feet high. They gathered, processed, and ate wild onions, wild sweet potatoes, and roots, such as the flat tule, which was boiled or roasted and then dried and pulverized. They consumed grasses, herbs, and many varieties of wild berries along with wild plums, grapes, and other native fruits. Few edible plants were not utilized for food.

Central to all of these activities were baskets. Baskets were necessary for gathering, collecting, and storage. U.S. Army Lieutenant George Derby reported in 1849, while camped in Nisenan territory, that a village of about 300 Nisenan people had "just commenced the collection for their winter stock of acorns, and had many high baskets, containing probably 40 or 50 bushels of this species of provender lying about." Woven cradleboards were used to hold and carry infants, and baskets were also used for cooking. Watertight baskets were filled with water and then rocks heated in a fire pit were dropped into the basket and stirred with sticks, carefully avoiding the sides of the basket. Eventually, after a few rocks had been used and then removed, the water would boil and cooking would be accomplished.

Local Nisenan baskets feature designs from nature, such as the "quail topknot" design on the right. Baskets were used for food preparation and cooking, with a hot "pot stone."

Women gathered material for basket-making all year long. Willow and redbud were the most common materials. They also used hazel, yellow pine roots, and fern stems. All Nisenan girls learned to make baskets. Basketry was utilitarian and essential to the gathering economy of the Nisenan and reached artistic levels that are still greatly admired today.

While women provided the community with carbohydrates through gathering, processing, and storing acorns, men provided protein for the community through fishing and hunting. As mentioned above, salmon provided the largest source of protein. Due to the extraordinary numbers of salmon that migrated up the Sacramento and Feather rivers each year, it was more efficient for the men to use nets, rather than hooks, for capturing fish. Other types of fish were also netted or speared. Nisenan men also hunted the pronghorn antelope and the tule elk with bow and arrow on the valley floor. The antelope was difficult to hunt due to its nimbleness and cautious nature, while the elk could be elusive since it was able to take refuge in tule ponds. Deer were not common on the valley floor. Their range was limited to the edges of the valley. The grizzly bear was almost always avoided by hunters and the community at large, but black bears were hunted by organized groups of village men. During the winter months, waterfowl was abundant and provided an additional source of protein.

In regard to the world at large, the Nisenan had few contacts beyond their local areas. Contact with other tribelets, or groups of affiliated villages, was limited to trade, shared ceremonies, and infrequent warfare. Trade was conducted by men, but it was unlikely that any man traveled more than twenty miles in any direction in his lifetime. A woman's knowledge of landmarks did not extend beyond six or seven miles in any direction. The world of the Nisenan was small and intimate. They had little knowledge of the greater world beyond the Sierra Nevada and the Coast Range, nor did they know of the San Joaquin Valley or of the Sacramento Valley north of modern-day Chico, but they knew every aspect of their own territory and the characteristics of that environment.

Such a small world required every person in the community to behave carefully and in great consideration of others. In their personal relationships, the Nisenan people were always careful and circumspect, never leaving any word or gesture to chance. Theodora Kroeber described the California Indian as,

...an introvert, reserved, contemplative, and philosophical. The promoter, the boaster, the aggressor, the egoist, the innovator, would have been looked at askance. The ideal was the man of restraint, dignity, rectitude, he of the Middle Way.

The "Middle Way" that Kroeber refers to lay at the core of Nisenan life. The Middle Way spoke not only of the community's world view, but also of the composure and actions of each person within the community on a daily basis. The Middle Way was a life that emphasized the denial of excess, particularly in reference to the physical world. Greed, egotistical behavior, or individualism separated one from the community and was not only dangerous but also potentially catastrophic. The hunter did not eat his own kill and the dancer did not create new steps or gestures and the storyteller did not change the story. This deep conservatism may be partly explained from an environmental perspective. The close quarters in which these people lived certainly required politeness and courtesy. In a village of only a few hundred inhabitants, one unruly person could cause chaos. There were also other factors at work that dictated against excess. As a non-agrarian people, the Nisenan depended on local resources that could not be increased at will. The Valley oak provided generously, but at static levels over three-year cycles. The salmon run was also generous, but it too was static. The first imperative of human life, sufficient food, had to be observed carefully. Nature could not be offended, for it controlled human life, and the Nisenan were wise enough to appreciate this over-arching reality.

All plants, animals, rivers, and mountains possessed spirits. Humans were entitled to use the natural resources around them, but were required to supplicate the spirits of whatever they used. Supplication took the form of ritual and ceremony. Hunters engaged in purification rituals that consisted of bathing, standing in cleansing smoke, and abstaining from sexual activity. During this preparation and during the hunt, they were solicitous of the animal's feelings and welfare. The cleansing ritual not only removed human body odors, giving the hunter greater efficacy, but also appeased the animal they hunted. The animal's spirit was now willing to give up its body for human use.

Certain rituals and ceremonies involved the entire community. These were usually held at a particular time each year.

The infrequency of warfare in the mid-Sacramento Valley region during this time indicates there was nearly always an ample food supply for the population living in the Valley. The acorn/salmon complex mitigated against war and in favor of cooperation. Indeed, food was so ample that villages hosted other villages in order to demonstrate their wealth and generosity. Since war was uncommon, it was not integrated into the social fabric of the culture of the Nisenan.

Environmental factors in the form of abundant food resources had a profound impact on the Nisenan. They lived peaceful and generally prosperous lives, with only about twenty hours of work required from each adult each week. The climate was mild, but punctuated by seasonal change, so, if the heat of the summer was too much, one only had to wait a while for the cool breezes of autumn. Likewise, if the cold and fog of winter became troublesome, then spring was not too far away. For over 3,000 years, the Nisenan people lived in the mid-Sacramento Valley region with little difficulty and in great balance with their environment. The Middle Way served them well. This mode of life, however, came to a tragic end when outsiders, culturally much more aggressive and bearing infectious diseases, began to arrive in the early 1800s. By the fifth decade of the century, the Nisenan would be nearly completely dispossessed of their mid-Sacramento Valley homeland.

Yuba City
FOUNDING YUBA CITY

Children play near the burned-out shell of the Sutter County Courthouse on Second Street in 1899. It was rebuilt according to the same plans and still stands today.

Imagine William Armstrong and his wife as they trudged along in the dark, pelted by a hard rain, making their way through the bottomlands next to the Feather River.

There were plenty of bears and large wolves in the river bottoms in 1849. They walked the last seven or eight miles to reach Yuba City, because they had no place to sleep. When they finally arrived at about ten o'clock that night, they found that Yuba City consisted of Mrs. Linder's tent, where they found refuge and a half-pole, half-canvas tent erected by Rolfe and Cheever, the town's first storekeepers.

Tallman Rolfe and David Cheever, as agents of the owners of the town lots, offered William Armstrong two lots if he would build a house on one. He agreed and built the first house in Yuba City of oak clapboards. In the spring, he put in a floor that cost $500 per thousand feet. In his memoirs, he remembered, "Every night after the house was built, men would come and offer to pay a dollar a night to sleep on the floor. Travelers, I mean of course. In Feb. 1850 I started the first ferry at Yuba City and my first job was ferrying over the packs of thirty-five mules. I had a whale boat to use for a ferry."

On July 27, 1849, John Sutter deeded 640 acres to himself, Sam Brannan, Pierson Reading, and Henry Cheever. This land lay on the west bank of the Feather River opposite the mouth of the Yuba River. The founders hired surveyor Joseph Ruth to lay out the town of Yuba City. This site on high ground near the river had also been recognized considerably earlier as a favorable location by the Yubu village of Nisenan Maidu, but their residence on the land was disregarded as Brannan and his partners hastened to establish the new town. Lots were being sold and tents were going up in Yuba City by the time the sleepy little settlement of Nye's Ranch across the river was laid out as the city of Marysville in January 1850.

By the spring of 1850, a great many tents were clustered on the riverbank at Yuba City. Stores, saloons, gambling houses, and residences filled the tent city. There was even a "tenpins bowling saloon." D. M. Hanson described Yuba City as "not a pretty town by any means, being constructed out of the odds and ends of anything that would cast a shadow; old tin cans, tenting, a little lumber, shakes, etc." Hanson described the four-mile-long by one-mile-wide plot of land that comprised the 640-acre area set aside for Yuba City: "Immediately below the conference of the rivers, there were rapids, in which the waters were shallow and the current was very strong, making navigation quite difficult. Below those rapids the Lower Yuba City was born while above them the Upper Town. Between the Upper and Lower towns was a large Indian rancheria containing hundreds of Indians."

By 1852, Yuba City consisted of one hotel, the Western House, one small grocery store, two saloons, one blacksmith shop, one justice of the peace, a post office, fifteen or twenty houses, and a population of 150. In spring of 1853, Reverend A. S. Brown established the Elkhorn House. That year saw the addition of another store and blacksmith shop to the growing village.

As the rush for gold boomed, it became apparent that Yuba City was on the wrong side of the Feather River for access to the goldfields. Many residents moved across the river to Marysville, which grew rapidly as a main supply point for the northern mines. *The Herald*, on April 19, 1851, painted this picture of the bustling new center:

Over one thousand mules loaded out of the Plaza alone in one day. Yesterday four steamers left our landing at nearly the same time, while one was coming in. There are now about eight or nine steamers plying here regularly from Sacramento City, and three from San Francisco direct. They all come loaded down with goods.

Edward Cheever, brother of Yuba City founder Henry Cheever and original storekeeper David Cheever, shed light on the origin of the name "Yuba." According to Earl Ramey in the Sutter County Historical Society *Bulletin*: "The name of Yuba City was spelled Yubu City on the first map of the townsite, this being done to preserve the original Indian name of the rancheria which also gave its name to the river. The Indians, however, pronounced the name Yubum (Youboom) and the village at Hock Farm was Hockem. But the newcomers changed the names to Yuba and Hock without regard to Indian origin or original pronunciation."

A letter to the editor from John Sutter appeared in *The Herald* on August 30, 1850:

Mr. Editor: . . . The name of your county is derived as follows: In the year 1840 I started with a party on an exploring expedition up the valley. Little was then known of this country above the mouth of the Feather River. I found along the valley many Indian tribes. I was particular to inquire of each tribe the name by which they were known and many other important matters which I carefully noted down in a book kept for that purpose together with the situation of the rancherias of each. The tribe I found at and which still remains at the old rancheria at Yuba City informed me that the name of their tribe was YUBU (pronounced YUBOO). As this tribe lived opposite the mouth of the river from which your county takes its name, I gave that river the name YUBU which it has ever since borne. Hence you discover that the river does not derive its name from the Spanish name of the vines which shroud its banks, nor is the name of that river YUBA or UBA as my friend Vallejo supposes but YUBU which cannot be derived from UVAS.

Yours truly,

J. A. Sutter

Eventually, some of the gold-seekers tried their hands at farming the rich Sutter County soil, and Yuba City slowly began to grow again.

Our present city does not follow the original plan laid out by surveyor Joseph Ruth. He plotted First through Thirteenth streets to parallel the Feather River, with cross streets named alphabetically. There were no levees, and boats tied up at the bank on Water Street, which logically should have been named First Street. Rolfe and Cheever set up their tent store in August 1849, about where the county office building is now, on the block bound by Second, B, and C streets. Water Street was the east boundary of that block, but it is now under the levee. Three wood houses were built on Water Street facing the river by April 1850. The Western Hotel was located at Water and B streets, and the landing for the first ferry was located opposite the hotel.

The general assumption was that Yuba City would grow to the south, because a slough formed a diagonal barrier across the northwest area of the city. That slough eventually took on the name of John Gelzhauser, a Marysville butcher, who built a slaughterhouse about a mile north of Yuba City. Over time, the name has evolved into Gilsizer Slough. Bridge Street no doubt was named for the very early rudimentary bridge that citizens put over the slough to enable travel to the West. That bridge preceded the first bridge over the Feather River, although Bridge Street also aligned with the series of bridges over the river. However, Yuba City grew to the north. Hudson's Addition was laid out in 1869, and contained six squares dissected by Sonoma, Solano, Yolo, Sutter, and Second streets.

In the spring of 1850, the citizens of the new town elected Harvey Fairchild alcalde. He served until the courts were organized in June. The landowners, in addition to Brannan, Reading, and Cheever, were Fairchild, storekeeper Tallman Rolfe, Henry A. Schoolcraft, George Pierson, W. S. Messick, Richard N. Allen, Jonas Winchester, Gordon N. Mott, George Hanson, W. S. Webb, and John Sutter's son, Emil V. Sutter.

On September 18, 1849, the four founding partners of Yuba City deeded certain lots to each other as individuals, each owner then selling or disposing of his land as he wished. Sam Brannan made a memorable gift in 1858, when he deeded Lots 1 and 2 of Block 18 in the Yuba City Tract to Sutter County to be used for the county courthouse. That is where the courthouse remains today.

Nisenan and Settlers— Contact and Removal

D. M. Hanson, in *Recollections of Hon. D. M. Hanson Crossing the Plains in '49*, describes the Indians of the Yubu village as he remembers them from childhood:

There were many Indians in Yuba City at that time living in a large rancharia between the Upper and Lower towns and we boys had many battles with the young redskins. Their dances on festival occasions were most interesting.

Fancifully dressed in feathers covering head and loins, the rest of their anatomy being unclad, they would squat and vault and pound the earthen floor with naked feet and indulge all kinds of acrobatic gyrations while keeping time with the bone whistle of the dancers, beating of tom-toms and the singing of the squaws which was not at all unmusical. The bucks alone did the dancing while the squaws sang, weaved scarfs and swung back and forth in rhythmical motion keeping time with the crude music. The bucks often had unique appurtenances attached to them representing birds and animals. Wings of the eagle and the horns of the elk and deer were often in evidence. These dances would last for a week or more and until provisions were exhausted, Indians gathering from long distances to attend them. Often they wound up with the "pole dance" which was a very interesting exercise. A long pine tree, perhaps 80 feet in length, barked and well seasoned, painted in Indian style in squares and angles in various colors by mineral and vegetable pigments of fast colors, was taken by the bucks on either side thereof, fancifully appareled, dancing, blowing whistles and beating of the tom-tom, at a signal from Wauketau, the chief, a quick run and plunge into the river was made, the river crossed and return made to the place from which it was taken amid deafening shouts and song. There was a significance to this dance which I've forgotten but it was a purposeful appeal of some kind to the Great Spirit. Another ceremony of invocation comes to memory wherein the Medicine Man would sit atop the council house ... and for hours harange the Great Spirit in a loud monotone invoking the blessings of good harvests of penola (wild wheat), acorns, game and fish. Many nights when a boy I have been lulled to sleep by the sonorous sound of that Priestly prayer.

Wauketau was the last chief of the Yubu village. The district of historic homes on the west side of Second Street is built on the site of the village. Wauketau became known because of his activities resisting the relocation of the village inhabitants to the Nome Lackee reservation in Tehama County, southwest of the town of Tehama.

The "Yuba City Indians" became a source of concern for citizens of both Yuba City and Marysville. Most of the Indians who occupied the present site of Marysville had been dispersed by white settlement, either into the foothills or to Yuba City. As the Yuba City Indians began to adapt to urban life, they would go across the river to Marysville to seek work or gifts of food, clothing, or money. Residents suspected them of petty thefts, and public sentiment on both sides of the river favored their removal. Unprincipled whites sold them liquor, and one rationalization for removal was that the Indians would be spared that temptation and would live in better conditions on the reservation. Perhaps removal also spared the settlers any uncomfortable feelings about having displaced the original residents.

In 1856, Colonel Thomas Henley, Indian agent for California, and John Sutter engaged in negotiations regarding removal with Wauketau and the leaders of the Hock, Oloi, and Olash villages. Sutter tried to convince them of the many advantages of going to Nome Lackee. A month later, the Indians were forcibly rounded up and held in the Marysville jail until they were taken to Yuba City to be handed over to the Indian agent. Then, the group of sixty-six was sent down the Feather River on the boat *Cleopatra* to Sacramento, where they were transferred to another boat for the trip up the Sacramento River to Tehama.

The Indians unanimously resisted their removal. They did not want to leave their home. Wauketau poignantly said they did not want to die somewhere else. When they understood that they were forced to go, they burned their houses.

Of the sixty-six Indians who were removed, thirty-six were men, twenty were women, and ten were children. There were no old people and no children over the age of eight. A probable explanation for the absence of older children is that the courts could legally bind children into service of a white family, a practice remarkably similar to slavery. It is known that there were children in Marysville held in that circumstance.

It is not surprising that the Indians were not happy on the reservation, and most eventually drifted back to this area. But they were never able to return to their ancestral villages or to their traditional way of life. Over time, their presence declined until there was almost no visible evidence of them having lived for thousands of years on the bank of the Feather River.

Becoming the County Seat

For many of us, it comes as a surprise that the location of the county seat was a hard-fought battle that lasted for several years. The first choice for a county seat was the community of Oro on the Bear River. The first meeting of the Court of Sessions of Sutter County opened at Oro on June 10, 1850. The first entry in the record reveals that the officers present, Gordon N. Mott as chief justice, P. W. Thomas and T. H. Rolfe as associate justices, and T. B. Reardon as clerk, recognized that there were no buildings at Oro that could serve as offices for the county officers, who were required by law to have open offices at the county seat. The nearest community with proper office space was Nicolaus, and so the next meeting took place in that town.

A few months later, after holding an election, the county seat moved to Auburn, which was then in Sutter County. The state legislature finished off Auburn's historic role in Sutter County when, in 1851, they created Placer County, part of which was carved off the Sutter County boundary. Auburn became the county seat of Placer County and Sutter County's officers began looking for a new home. The new boundaries of the county were set on April 25, 1851, and the legislature named Vernon as county seat. At that time, one of the proprietors of Vernon, E. O. Crosby, was also the state senator for the district, which was probably the reason for Vernon's selection.

However, Vernon's time in the spotlight was brief when, on May 3, 1852, due to considerable alterations to the county's boundaries and the fact that Vernon was nearly deserted, the county seat moved once more to Nicolaus. In 1854, supporters of Yuba City pushed for an election so the people could decide where the county seat should be. Nicolaus won that election, but it was contested. Supporters of Yuba City claimed that illegal voting practices occurred at Johnson's Crossing. They claimed that teamsters, stage drivers, and travelers who were making the crossing that day, but didn't live in Sutter County, were allowed to vote. If the Johnson's Crossing votes were tossed out, then Yuba City supporters won the day. The ruling must have been favorable to Yuba City, as the February 1855 term of court was held there. But, to add to the confusion, the August 1855 term of court was back in Nicolaus. Finally, on June 10, 1856, the Board of Supervisors ordered that all archives and moveable property be taken to Yuba City, and the county seat has remained in this place ever since.

Sutter County was without a jail or a courthouse at this time, and the decision was made to construct both in Yuba City. With a location on Second Street between B and C streets donated by Sam Brannan, construction commenced, and the building was completed and accepted by the county on September 18, 1856. This building served its function well, but, on December 23, 1871, the *Sutter County Banner* reported that the "Court House is in Ashes."

Authorized by the state legislature to raise funds to build and furnish another courthouse and jail, the supervisors were directed to levy and collect a tax to create a special fund known as the Courthouse Fund. The rate was not to exceed fifty cents on each one hundred dollars of taxable property. This, along with borrowing money from the Swamp Land Fund, was approved by the legislature and passed on February 2, 1872. On April 3, 1872, the building contract was signed, construction begun, and on December 12, 1872, the county officers moved into the new building even though some finishing work was still being done.

Except for adding a basement, no changes were made to the courthouse until it once again had to be rebuilt after another disastrous fire in April 1899.

One last bid was made to move the county seat to Sutter City, but the construction of the current courthouse put it to rest.

AGRICULTURE

Yuba City

Agriculture was Yuba City's lifeblood for most of its existence. Unlike Marysville, Yuba City's base was not commercial. Its economy has always been based on agriculture.

Yuba City was surrounded right up to its borders with orchards and crops. Incorporated within the town were packinghouses, dry yards, and canneries. Agricultural warehouses abutted commercial and residential areas. Many people in Yuba City worked for agriculture-related businesses. The canneries employed women and even children.

In the 1860s, wheat was the biggest crop in Sutter County. Much of the grain was shipped out by riverboat, and large warehouses sprang up along the riverbank in Yuba City. In 1873, local farmers formed the Farmers' Cooperative Union. It was a marketing cooperative that sought better prices for their crops, built a warehouse to store wheat before shipment, and loaned surplus funds back to the farmers. This led to the

Farmers load fruit onto railroad cars at Bogue Station in 1914.

Rosenberg Brothers and Company at the corner of B and Shasta streets processed dried fruit and beans and later went into canning.

LOADEL IS A PEACH

Howard Harter liked to experiment with extra early varieties of canning peaches. In the 1940s, he discovered a new peach variety growing as a sprout in one of the experimental trees. It turned out that this new peach had a wonderful taste similar to freestone peaches, but it was a cling with a small, easily removed pit, making it ideal for canning. He developed the peach and named it after his daughter Loadel. The first Loadel Peach trees were ready for sale in 1955. Unfortunately, they were lost in the 1955 flood, so he had to begin propagation all over again. If you are fortunate enough to find Loadel Peaches at a farmer's market or roadside stand, be sure to give yourself a taste treat. Loadel Harter Piner recommends it.

creation of the Farmers' Union Bank in Yuba City. In 1912, it became the First National Bank of Yuba City, located at the corner of Bridge and Sutter streets. The Yuba City Flour Mill, built by John Wilkie, also at Sutter and Bridge streets, began production in 1875, producing one hundred barrels of flour daily.

Farmers began turning to fruit orchards, such as peaches, and, after the Thompson Seedless Grape was developed by George Thompson in 1872, they put large acreages into grapes. The first railroad carload of fruit was shipped from California to eastern markets from the John Briggs orchard just south of Yuba City in 1876.

John Paxton Onstott propagated the Thompson Seedless Grape, selling it to nurseries as far away as Fresno and Los Angeles. He farmed more than 1,000 acres in Sutter County, with 800 planted to Thompson Seedless Grapes. With his brother Jacob, they dried grapes and were the first to ship them by rail to eastern markets. He is known as the father of the raisin industry. Onstott Freeway, which traverses his former holdings, is named in his honor.

In May 1883, B. F. Walton headed a group of growers that founded the Sutter Canning and Packing Company to meet the need for a processing plant, which they built at B Street and Wilbur Avenue. In 1888, Joseph Phillips developed the Phillips Cling Peach, ideal for canning, and it spurred the rapid growth of the canning industry.

By the last decades of the nineteenth century, farmers were farming smaller acreages more intensively than formerly when wheat was the main crop, producing peaches, prunes, cherries, pears, olives, apricots, figs, plums, apples, nectarines, and nuts.

Above: Fairs have been held on the Yuba-Sutter Fairgrounds since 1941. Carolyn (Oswald) Mock was crowned Miss Peach in 1947 and represented the Yuba-Sutter Fair at the State Fair's Centennial Girl Contest.

Right: This postcard advertised the local area as "The Peach Bowl of the World." It is likely a photo of Yuba and Sutter counties' entry at the State Fair, circa 1930.

Rosenberg Brothers opened their Yuba City cannery in 1889, just across the railroad tracks from the first cannery. In 1900, Hunt Brothers bought out both Rosenberg and Sutter Canning and Packing. The Sutter Preserving Company built a new cannery on B Street in 1903, but it soon failed financially. Eventually, the plant was bought by Central California Cannery and its name changed to the California Packing Company, or C.P.C.

Harter Packing Company opened on Harter Road west of Yuba City in 1927. In 1969, it became a division of CHB Foods; in 1988, Harter, Inc., was sold and closed in 2001.

By the 1920s, Yuba-Sutter produced half of the world's canning peaches. Sutter County became renowned as "The Peach Bowl of the World," but it also produced plums, cherries, almonds, grapes, figs, beans, grain, and rice. However, a lethal grape pest called phylloxera killed most of the grape vines in the mid-1920s.

At mid-century, rice was established as Sutter County's main crop, producing 72,600 tons in 1950. Agricultural industries were Sunsweet, Inc., for dried prunes, Golden Empire Walnut Growers, Earle Fruit Company (Di Giorgio), Yuba City Refrigerating Company, Sacramento Freezers, Inc., Northrup King & Company, and Yuba City Mills.

AGRICULTURE BROUGHT DIVERSITY

Immigrants from all over the world arrived in California to make a new life. Many, like the Chinese, arrived during the Gold Rush era of the 1850s and stayed on. Others, like the Punjabis and Japanese, came just before and after the turn of the twentieth century. Immigrants included Filipinos, Southern Europeans, Mexicans, and refugees from the Dust Bowl. The Sikhs from the Punjab came to help build roadbeds for the Northern Electric Railway, but stayed to farm. The common thread that ran among all of the groups was agriculture. Most of them knew farming from their native lands, and they wanted to farm the rich soil of Sutter County.

Both the Chinese and Japanese kept sizeable gardens on the outskirts of early Yuba City, which provided fresh produce to the

HARTER BOYS' PEACH ICE CREAM

About half a freezer full of freestone peaches, mashed and put through a colander

4 eggs, beaten

Lemon juice and sugar to taste

Pour into a 3-quart freezer, and fill to the proper level with milk.

This recipe belonged to the four Harter boys, Orlin Jr., Dick, James and Jerry, and to their grandmother, Mrs. Clyde Harter. It wasn't really a recipe, but more in the nature of a boyish experiment, for they would throw things together and taste to see if they had the right amount. Jerry, the youngest, would sit on top of the freezer while his brothers would turn the crank. They turned it until it was as hard as they could get it, and usually about half of the ice cream would come out with the dasher. This was their reward for turning the crank.

Esther Harter

(Courtesy of Loadel Piner)

Yesterday & Today: A Heritage of Cooking in Sutter & Yuba Counties

Community Memorial Museum

residents of the town. A Japanese immigrant, Mr. Ikuta, introduced rice-growing to the area around 1910.

Many area residents were distressed when their Japanese American neighbors were forced to leave their homes to go to detention camps during World War II. Many were sent to Tule Lake or Camp Amache in Colorado, taking only what they could carry. At the war's end, they returned to find that they had lost their homes and farms. Some discovered that their neighbors had cared for their properties, but most had to begin again.

The rich diversity of Yuba City today is a direct result of agriculture. These groups continue their interest in farming, contributing to our community in unique ways.

Mule teams deliver grain to Yuba City Milling Company at Bridge and Shasta streets.

A photo from the Farm Security Administration pictures farm worker housing on Garden Highway. It is described as "Farm Workers' Community, Yuba City, Cal. 1940… Two-story house-rows grouped about a pecan grove in a minimum-cost rural housing project of extraordinary distinction."

The Cooper Cutting Shed was located at the corner of Bridge Street and Cooper Avenue around 1910. Cut fruit was laid out on drying trays in the sun.

"Hauss Clings Are Now on Display"
The Marysville Appeal, July 29, 1914

There is on exhibition in the Chamber of Commerce window on Second Street a sample of the "Hauss Cling Peaches", which is attracting considerable attention. The Hauss Cling peach was propagated eighteen years ago by F. Hauss in a nursery at Oswald. The peach has already become desirable by the cannery men, and this year the price for the fruit was $2.50 per ton more than the Tuscan Cling was sold for.

Mr. Hauss after discovering that his propagation was successful immediately budded all the young nursery stock possible to obtain buds from the parent tree and planted all the trees raised on his orchard at Oswald, and as a result he now has five acres of seven-year-old trees which will bear their first heavy crop next year.

The principal features of the Hauss cling peach are that it is a midsummer cling and ripens immediately after the Tuscan clings are gathered; that it is a firm canner, does not discolor the syrup, being a yellow peach to the pit; that it has an excellent and a distinct flavor which can be distinguished readily from any other peach. An important feature is that it has a very small pit. It has already proved to be a very heavy and almost certain bearer.

Workers sort and pack fresh cherries in a packinghouse, circa 1920. Cherries were a major local crop in the first decades of the twentieth century.

Ferdinand Hauss

Yuba City
BURNING TO INCORPORATE

THE EARLIEST ATTEMPT

When you read the history of nearly any community in the nineteenth century, it becomes clear that fire devastated town after town.

The melancholy pall is almost tangible after the 1907 fire on Second Street.

By 1877, Yuba City had seen its share of fires, and businessmen and other property owners were examining their options. Specifically, they wanted to have public protection from fire and improvements to the town's infrastructure. At this point, Yuba City did not have a fire department or fire fighting equipment of its own. In order to pay for these improvements, a more formal government that had the power to write and enforce ordinances, as well as levy and collect taxes, needed to be created.

In order to accomplish this, a bill for incorporation was introduced and passed by the state legislature and approved by Governor William Irwin on March 30, 1878. The Act called for the formation of an elected three-man Board of Trustees and one assessor. They were to appoint a marshal and were given the power to levy a tax not exceeding 0.5 percent and a poll tax of one dollar and were not allowed to accrue any debt.

An election for the Board of Trustees resulted in W. F. Peck, S. J. Stabler, and J. B. Stafford being elected to fill the Board. A. E. Clary was elected assessor. In accordance with the charter, these men met within ten days of the election to organize the new city.

At the first meeting, after examining their budget and their needs and recognizing their lack of ability to meet their obligations without accruing debt, they soon realized that they could not fund a fire department or the other planned improvements. The Board decided to abandon the attempt to incorporate the city. Interested citizens tried to raise money by subscription to pay for fire protection apparatus, but their efforts failed as well, and it would be another thirty years before incorporation and local fire protection prevailed.

We have a description of Yuba City from this time in Thompson & West's *History of Sutter County*, published in 1879:

> At the present time Yuba City contains one Court House, two churches, one school house, one Masonic Hall, one Brewery, four warehouses, one flouring mill, one general store, one drug store, two grocery stores, nine saloons, one meat market, one barber shop, one confectionery store, one hotel, one livery stable, three blacksmith and wagon shops, one post office, five attorneys, two physicians, one weekly newspaper, about seventy dwelling houses and a population of about 600.

CONFLAGRATION

Yuba City faced a number of challenges in 1907. A flood in March damaged the bridge linking Yuba City with Marysville. A nationwide weak economy led to the Bank Panic of 1907. Some businesses, including Rideout Bank and the Northern Electric Railroad, were issuing scrip for a time. In October of this eventful year came the local catastrophe which would result in incorporation for Yuba City.

On October 4, 1907, fire swept through the heart of downtown Yuba City. Nearly the entirety of commercial Second Street burned when a fire began in the Windsor Hotel, which was located on the west side of Second Street between Bridge and Fairman streets.

The fire started in the hotel kitchen when the cook improperly started the oil-burning stove. Beginning at about four o'clock in the

LOSSES

While most of the losses listed are commercial, many of these owners of the buildings rented out rooms on unused floors; therefore, the personal losses of these men are unrecorded.

The Windsor House, a two-story brick hotel

Law offices of A. H. Hewitt, a two-story cement building

Odd Fellows Building, a two-story brick building, with the lower floor occupied by E. G. Van Arsdale's grocery store, and the upper portion used for lodge purposes

Valley Meat Company, located in the hotel building

J. E. Jones's barbershop

Dr. A. E. Kosby's two-story frame building, occupied as office and residence

C. P. Slattery Estate's two-story brick building, with lower floor used by Best & Willitson, grocers, and upper portion used by Vernon White as a residence

Slattery Estate & J. K. P. Elwell, two-story frame building, with lower floor occupied by N. C. Hull, barber, and D. A. Mount, painter, and upper floor devoted to Dr. Cole's offices

Annex to Masonic Hall, with downstairs used by Union Ice Company, and upper floor used by Masons for anterooms, etc.

Yuba City Water Company's plant and buildings

Orr & Wilcoxon's blacksmith shop

O. Moncur's two-story frame and corrugated building, with first floor used by a tinsmith, and upper floor to have been devoted to residence purposes, but not completed

Williams Brothers' livery and feed stables

C. H. Potter's residence

Billiard parlor

S. J. Stabler's law offices

Jones Insurance

Sutter County Chamber of Commerce

Five barns

Minor damage to the Yuba City Post Office, the store of McRae & Ashley, and the newspaper building

afternoon, the spread of the fire was aided by a strong north wind. The fire quickly spread to engulf nearly the entire west side of Second Street from the Masonic Temple at the corner of Bridge and Sutter streets to B Street to the south. It jumped Second Street, caught the town's water tower on fire, and quickly brought it down. The only fire fighting equipment in Yuba City at the time was a handcart and hose that was stored beneath the water tower. Nearly the entire business district in Yuba City was destroyed.

Some owners had insurance, but without a fire department for protection, insurance was expensive. It does not appear that any of the owners or business people were completely covered for their losses. Attorney A. H. Hewitt's fireproof safe proved to be of little use when he rushed over to close it and found that, in his absence, others had stacked books in the vault and blocked the door from closing. While he managed to escape his office with smoke inhalation and burns to his hands and neck, all of the important documents in the vault burned.

The crowd at Second and Bridge streets watches as the main business district burns on October 2, 1907.

Losses spread beyond property owners and businessmen. Many of the structures were dual-purpose, serving as both businesses and housing. Even the bottom floor of the water tower served as living quarters. For the people living in these rented rooms and apartments, the fire meant the loss of all of their possessions.

People came out by the hundreds to watch the blaze, and volunteers worked to keep the fire from spreading onto Bridge Street. The manager of the Yuba City C.F.C.A., a local fruit canning plant, closed shop and took about fifty men down to the fire and positioned them at every residence that was in line with the fire to protect them. Salvation came in the form of the Marysville Fire Department, which sent an engine, hose cart, and chemical wagon to Yuba City. The engine was backed up to the levee, and water was pumped out of the Feather River. Throughout the night, Marysville firemen and local volunteers kept an eye on the fire, putting out spot fires as they occurred. Without the aid of the Marysville firemen and volunteers, losses would have been much greater. In appreciation for their help, local businessmen dug deep into their pockets and made a handsome donation to the Marysville Fire Department.

With the city's main water source destroyed, the Rosenberg Packing House stepped in and connected the company's water supply to the B Street main and furnished 20,000 gallons of water a day to Yuba City to tide residents over until the water company could set up pumps in the Feather River.

Fortunately, there were no deaths due to the fire, and the injuries suffered were minor, the most serious coming from a fall when the porch of the Masonic Temple collapsed under the weight of firefighters who were using the space to stage an assault on the nearby fire.

REACTION TO CRISIS

Residents and businessmen in Yuba City reacted as many do after a life-changing event. Most of the businesses began rebuilding immediately. Some closed permanently in Yuba City and relocated to other towns. Those that could found quarters elsewhere until their new buildings were completed. Those who rebuilt took measures to insure that their stores could stand up to fire better than the wooden buildings that made up so much of downtown Yuba City.

Immediately in the aftermath of the fire, discussions about incorporating the town arose. With incorporation would come civil services: a fire department, public waterworks, a police department, etc. The first meeting called to discuss incorporation occurred on October 9, 1907, at the Sutter County Courthouse. Over one hundred people met at the courthouse and appointed a commission to present a petition requesting the Sutter County Board of Supervisors call for a special election so the citizens could vote on incorporation and set the boundaries of the proposed town. Or, as the *Daily Appeal* put it:

All who attended the meeting in the crowded Superior court room were decidedly in favor of incorporation and the greatest little town in Northern California, which has been held back by a few sleepy citizens, will now rise from its bed of ashes and go ahead with a vim and swing that will be the envy of the other cities of the valley.

Several citizens spoke out in favor of incorporation including District Attorney Lawrence Schillig, Sheriff F. B. Noyes, J. E. Orr, O. Moncur, C. R. Boyd, C. E. McQuaid, C. B. Andross, A. S. Barr, C. E. Williams, C. D. O'Banion, Dr. A. E. Kosby, C. L. Wilbur, and A. A. McRae. C. L. Wilbur expressed concern about the "saloon question." Would a new city government undo the county ordinance that resulted in Sutter County being "dry" since 1891? The district attorney pointed out that "if the people elect Trustees who are not in favor of saloons, there will be no saloons."

A second mass meeting occurred for the incorporation committee to report their findings. The chairman of the committee, Lawrence Schillig, reported the committee found that the general law of the state was the best under which to proceed, keeping Yuba City in line with other local communities such as Gridley, Biggs, Wheatland, Lincoln, Colusa, and Auburn. The proposed boundaries were examined and accepted, and the resolution adopting the report was unanimously adopted.

Approval for an election was readily given by the Board of Supervisors, and the election was scheduled for January 14, 1908.

The Results
Daily Appeal, January 15, 1908

By a vote of 7 to 1 the electors of the district comprised within the proposed incorporate limits of Yuba City yesterday declared in favor of making a city out of the thrifty little Sutter county burg. There were 147 votes cast in favor of incorporation and but 21 votes cast against the

Yuba City residents examine damage in the business district from the previous day's fire.

NOTICE

—OF—

MUNICIPAL ELECTION

The Electors of the Town of Yuba City, County of Sutter, State of California, are hereby notified that at a regular meeting of the Board of Trustees of said Town held on Monday, the 16th day of March, 1908, the following call for a General Municipal Election was passed and adopted by resolution as follows:

Resolved, that a General Municipal Election be, and the same is hereby called to be held in the Town of Yuba City, County of Sutter, State of California, on

MONDAY, the 13th day of April, 1908

for the election of the following officers of the said Town of Yuba City, to-wit:

A Board of Trustees to consist of five members, provided that said Board so elected shall, at their first meeting, so classify themselves by lot as that three of their number shall go out of office at the expiration of two years and two at the expiration of four years;

Marshal for a term of two years;

Clerk for a term of two years;

Treasurer for a term of two years.

That the said election shall be conducted in accordance with the general election laws of the State, so far as the same may be made applicable.

That the two election precincts into which said Town of Yuba City has been divided for general State elections be, and the same are hereby consolidated into one election precinct for holding said Municipal Election, and the polling place therefor will be at the Williams Livery Stable on Second Street in said Town. The polls will open at six o'clock of the morning of the day of said Municipal Election and will be kept open until six o'clock in the afternoon of the same day, when the polls will be closed.

That the following named persons be and they are hereby appointed a Board of Election for said Municipal Election, to-wit:

Judges—Luther Ashley and J. F. Bickley;

Inspectors—E. T. Barrett and J. T. Hughes;

Clerks—E. M. Boyd and Arthur Coates;

Ballot Clerks—T. J. Holmes and C. A. Duncan.

That the compensation of each of said officers of said Board of Election be, and the same is hereby fixed at $3.00 per day.

Witness our hands this 17th day of March, 1908.

Attest:

[SEAL]

C. M. SHELDON,
Clerk of the Town of Yuba City.

J. W. ASHLEY,
President of the Board of Trustees.

proposal. The total number of votes cast was 187. Nineteen ballots were not counted as the proposition of incorporation was not voted for or against. Yuba City will now take her place among the municipalities of the state and there will be a growth and progress in the Sutter capital that will surprise even the most enthusiastic friends of the incorporation project.

Also decided that day were positions in the new government. Elected were W. H. Chism as marshal/tax collector, A. S. Barr as clerk/assessor, and C. R. Boyd as treasurer. E. G. Van Arsdale, J. H. Wilkie, J. W. Ashley, O. T. Boyd, and J. M. Kelly were elected as trustees.

At the first meeting of the Board of Trustees for Yuba City, Jay W. Ashley was elected the president of the Board, which entitled him to be called mayor, thus becoming the first mayor of Yuba City. The only other decision made at the meeting on January 27, 1908, was the ordinance setting the day and place of future meetings—the first Monday night of each month at the Board of Supervisors room in the Sutter County courthouse.

The Trustee Board began writing ordinances that shaped the development of Yuba City, with the second being a city ordinance to reassure those who feared Yuba City was in danger of becoming "wet." It prohibited selling liquor or gambling within the town limits to match the county ordinance that regulated the same. This position was reversed, however, as investment in rebuilding a hotel in Yuba City depended on the newly constructed establishment being able to sell liquor. With approval for this one saloon to operate in Yuba City, the city's twenty-five-year "dry spell" ended. Edward Von Geldern, a local engineer, remembered that on the opening day the hotel provided a free lunch in a circus-like atmosphere and that the tables extended out to the middle of Bridge Street. "Two tables were provided, one for the wets and one for the dries, but before the day was over, they were pretty mixed up."

Other ordinances followed, including the definition of fire limits in the downtown area and the prohibition against construction of wooden buildings within that vicinity. Business licenses came next, with controls

Daily Appeal,
January 17, 1908

It may seem that bills never stop arriving, but it's a rare bill that arrives before the existence of the client…

City Clerk A. S. Barr, who has as yet not been sworn in and will not assume the responsibilities of his office until after next Monday night, when the new city government will be organized, was today brought face to face with the nerve of a book publishing house. Mr. Barr received a bill made out against the city of Yuba City for a set of books ordered back in last August by a couple of local lawyers.

Clerk Barr is now satisfied that the stories he has read for years about the book agent and book printing people are correct. Here is an instance of where an effort is being made to collect a bill of an incorporation that did not exist when the bill was made out and for books never ordered, even, by the city's representative.

J. W. Ashley, first mayor of Yuba City

Firemen show off the Yuba City Fire Department trucks. The fire department was located beneath the water tower on Plumas Street in the 1930s.

over mundane businesses as well as circuses, bowling, auctions, door-to-door salesmen, hauling services, peddlers, skating rinks, and shooting galleries. Institutions created from ordinances include the waterworks, fire department, and police department.

The availability of water was the first thing voted on in incorporated Yuba City. In April 1908, during an election that voted in J. W. Ashley, G. T. Boyd, J. B. Wilkie, E. G. Van Arsdale, and J. Kelly for trustees, C. M. Sheldon for clerk, W. H. Chism for marshal, and C. R. Boyd for treasurer, the voting citizens of Yuba City voted for bonds to support a public waterworks, 112 to 6. The area to be served was restricted to Cooper and Robinson streets on the west, the Feather River on the east, Teegarden Avenue and Colusa Highway on the north, and B and C streets on the south. By May of 1909, the last contract, given to Pacific Gas and Electric to provide electricity to the pumping plant, was accepted by the trustees.

Two of the most enduring and important services to come out of incorporation were the development of the fire and police departments. Once incorporated, the town of Yuba City had the responsibility to provide protection for its inhabitants. The town constable, William H. Chism, was overwhelmingly elected town marshal and served from April 1908 to April 1910. The Town Council rented office space in the building at Bridge and Yolo streets and any miscreants who needed time in jail went to the county jail at the courthouse.

The fire department, a volunteer organization, received authorization for its first purchase in May 1909, when the trustees gave approval for the purchase of two nozzles, 500 feet of hose, and two hose carts. One cart was kept at the Diamond Match Company east of Shasta Street and south of Bridge Street, and the other was kept at the garage owned by Fire Chief Red McDowell at Second and Fairman streets.

Our City Council grew out of the Board of Trustees, and during this, our centennial year of incorporation, members include Mayor Rory Ramirez, Mayor Pro Tem Leslie McBride, Councilmember Kash Gill, Councilmember Tej Maan, and Councilmember John Miller.

Yuba City
TRANSPORTATION

The first official ferry crossing of the Feather River at Yuba City was established just above the mouth of the Yuba River in 1850 and was operated by Samuel Bayless and Sarshel Woods. However, earlier that year in February, William Armstrong operated a ferry business at Yuba City using a whaleboat.

The first bridge built across the Feather River was a "cheap truss bridge" erected by George Hanson in September 1853. It cost $20,000 to build, and a toll was charged to cross it. In 1854, it partially collapsed under the weight of a cattle drive and was repaired. Many supported the construction of a free bridge. The bridge owners lobbied against it, but Sutter County built a new bridge in 1861.

The new covered bridge, known as the Parks Bridge for its champion State Senator W. H. Parks, was located roughly where the Fifth Street Bridge crosses now. Its entrance was near the World War I Veterans Memorial Park at the end of Bridge Street, and it angled slightly across the river to meet the Fifth Street grade in Marysville. It was to be a free bridge, so it would require a toll only until the $30,000 construction expense was paid. With both bridges but 500 feet apart and charging a toll at that time, a great competition for the traffic arose.

Hanson's bridge collapsed a second time in 1861 with cattle crossing it and was again repaired, in time to be swept away in the flood of 1861–1862. The bridge broke apart as two teams were crossing it, and one man was slightly injured.

The bridge construction crew pauses for the photographer in 1861. The covered bridge connected Marysville and Yuba City over the Feather River until it made way for a new bridge in 1905.

The Parks Bridge became toll free in 1871. In 1905, the Northern Electric Company along with Yuba and Sutter counties erected a combination wagon and railroad bridge. Its construction was interrupted by the 1907 flood. Part of the old covered bridge remained until destroyed by floodwaters in 1909.

Two bridges currently carry traffic across the Feather River. The Tenth Street Bridge, on Highway 20, was dedicated on September 19,

1947. During the 1955 flood, a large section of the existing Fifth Street Bridge (Twin Cities Bridge) was washed away, as well as the railroad bridge next to it. Although the railroad bridge was rebuilt within nine months, the Fifth Street Bridge was not finished until May 1958.

Retired Highway Patrolman Hanlon Brown remembered stopping traffic on the Fifth Street Bridge so that cattle or sheep could be herded across the bridge.

Boathouse owners Elmer Jackson and Charles Young pose for photographer Clara Smith in front of the covered bridge, circa 1900.

"Heavy Traffic Over Bridge— Bridge Keeper Keeps Count of Travel Over the Feather River" *Marysville Appeal*, May 3, 1914

A count upon the number of vehicles, horses, cattle, automobiles, motorcycles and bicycles which cross the Feather river bridge during a period of eleven hours was kept yesterday by T.B. Wright, gatekeeper on the approach. . . . At the conclusion of the count the totals were as follows: Cattle, 15; loose head of horses, 10; horsemen, 8; automobiles, 413; buggies and wagons, 569; motorcycles, 40; bicycles, 146.

THE MARYSVILLE-YUBA CITY RAILROAD

The Marysville-Yuba City Railroad was the name given to the system of mule-drawn streetcars that connected the two towns beginning in 1889 and continuing through 1906. There were four cars, two open and two closed. The car barn and stable were on C and Oak streets in Marysville. The span of mules was hitched offset so that they would not walk on the rails.

Tom Peirano went to work as one of the drivers. According to his daughter, Winifred Peirano Greene, in the Sutter County Historical Society *Bulletin*, the drivers faced some challenges. One of the cars was held up at gunpoint by two robbers on B Street in Yuba City one night, and the five passengers were compelled to turn over their cash. Groups of boys would occasionally sneak up behind the car and try to derail it. One year, on April Fool's Day, a group of pranksters placed a dummy on the tracks. It spooked the mules, who ran over the "body," and the driver thought he had killed someone.

The bridge tender's cottage sits to the left of the entrance to the covered bridge on the Yuba City side of the Feather River, circa 1900.

Mrs. Greene remembered that "an inebriated gentleman who had tarried too long at The Cliff House on the Marysville side of the bridge was discovered badly mangled near the tracks and was presumed to have been run over by the car. According to a later account in a Marysville paper, he had recovered sufficiently to resume drinking."

The Northern Electric Railway

The Northern Electric Railway, incorporated in 1905, was California's longest interurban line, stretching from Chico to Oroville, south to Yuba City and Marysville, and in 1907, to Sacramento. The Yuba City section also ran to Colusa. It was a third-rail electric system, its power coming from a charged third rail. When the Northern Electric Railway began in 1905, they bought the mule-drawn railway and replaced it with electrically powered streetcar lines, serving the two cities until 1942, when the Twin Cities Transit bus line started.

The Northern Electric provided an efficient and convenient mode of travel for area residents between towns. Elizabeth Smith shared her

memories of the Northern Electric Railway in the July 2001 Sutter County Historical Society *Bulletin*.

A Northern Electric car pauses at the station on Bridge Street, circa 1909. Note the track in the foreground and to the left in photo.

Elizabeth Smith remembers the train well. As a small child, she lived near the track and saw the car make its daily trips. She rode the car to Sacramento, and later when she went to college she rode it to Chico.

The most memorable thing about the train was the movement of the cars. They rocked so much passengers had to hang on tightly to stay in their seats. The cars were regular large train cars, but they ran on electricity without an engine. Sometimes trains had two cars, sometimes three. She never saw who drove the train, but there was always a conductor to take the tickets.

She remembers it was funny when three train cars rode down the middle of D Street in Marysville.

The power was provided by the third rail, except in town, where there were overhead wires, and at road crossings, where there was a break in the rail. A long train would reach the other side and touch the rail again before the back end had lost its power; a short train had enough momentum to cross the intersection and pick up power again.

Despite the warnings about avoiding the third rail, Elizabeth knew boys with rubber soled tennis shoes who could jump onto the rail and then jump off again.

Free!  Free!

BREAKFAST FLIGHT

TO

"The Peach Bowl of the World"

Grand Opening
Yuba City Airport

Meet A Peach - Get A Peach

Sun. Aug. 31, 1947

Be Our Flying Guests for Breakfast and Entertainment

Breakfast Served from 9 A. M. to 11 A. M.

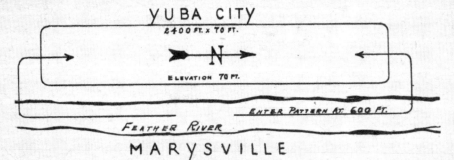

Sponsored By

Yuba-Sutter Flyers Incorporated

And

Sutter County Chamber of Commerce

The Northern Electric train depot, located on Bridge Street west of Plumas Street, is pictured on February 27, 1921.

By January 1909, the Northern Electric had put up a station at the end of Bridge Street. The flood of November 1909 took out the Northern Electric Bridge over the Feather River just after a train had passed over it. The reconstructed span was partially connected to the Feather River vehicular bridge.

The Northern Electric became the Sacramento Northern Railroad after a reorganization in 1918. Following a merger in 1928, it was known as the Sacramento Northern Railway. This interurban link between northern Central Valley towns and the state capitol and Bay Area served passengers until 1941. Increased automobile traffic and improved roads along with competing diesel railroads caused the decline of this convenient mode of travel.

IN THE SKIES

Yuba City has had three different airports over the years. According to aviation scholar Allen Herr in the Sutter County Historical Society *Bulletin*, likely the first place where airplanes landed in Yuba City was the very spot where the Sutter County Airport is today, on the southern end of Second Street near the levee. This area was known as Jackson Bottoms.

A transient aviator who landed in Jackson Bottoms one day in 1920 was Charles Kingsford-Smith, an Australian who later went on to become a famous long-distance flier known as "the Australian Lindbergh." He was out of gas and money, so the Von Geldern family invited him to stay in their home. He remained in Yuba

The Marysville-Yuba City open streetcar moves at a good clip behind the mule team, circa 1905.

City for a month or two, giving rides in his airplane for ten dollars.

The first airport in Yuba City was Angel Airport. It was located at the southwest corner of Colusa Highway and South Walton Avenue, where the Sam's Club parking lot is today. Jimmie Angel and the Angel Flying Circus performed at the 1926 Fourth of July celebration in Yuba City. Dr. Julian Johnson, founder of Johnson's Emergency Hospital on Plumas Street and an aviation fan, formed an agreement with Angel. Johnson leased land on the Glenn Onstott ranch, and Angel transferred his airplanes and employees from San Jose to Yuba City. The airport opened on August 8, 1926, when Jimmie Angel flew his Lincoln-Standard onto the field. Many area residents had their first exposure to aviation at Angel Airport. Sadly, Angel Airport was not long-lived. A powerful thunderstorm hit Yuba City on November 27 of that year, and wind tore off the hangar roof and damaged or destroyed most of the planes. Jimmie Angel left, and the airport closed. Angel went on to discover the world's tallest waterfall, Angel Falls, while flying in Venezuela.

The second airport sprang up five miles west of Yuba City on Township Road near Nuestro Road on land owned by E. F. Galbraith. Sutter Air Terminal, Inc., operated the airport, which opened on August 28, 1930, with a celebration that attracted 5,000 people and lasted five days. However, the airport faded into obscurity in a short time.

In 1945, aviation returned to Jackson Bottoms, when Levee District No. 1 and the Federal Farm Security Administration deeded 184 acres to Sutter County for an airport. In 1950, after completion of a new 2,040-foot runway, the airport was dedicated.

Charley Taylor and Bill Hines are pictured with Northern Electric Streetcar No. 28 that ran between Yuba City and Marysville.

JOHN J. MONTGOMERY, THE "FATHER OF AVIATION"

Yuba City was the birthplace of pioneer aviator John J. Montgomery in

A family waits for the mule-drawn trolley on the corner of Second and B streets around 1910. Tracks are visible in the foreground.

A Sacramento Northern car heads to Marysville in the 1940s.

1858. Montgomery made the first controlled-wing flight, at a distance of 600 feet, on August 28, 1883, from a hilltop near San Diego in a glider of his own design and manufacture. That landmark event took place twenty years before the Wright brothers' historic flight. In fact, the Wright brothers used some of Montgomery's research in their project. Montgomery became chair of the physics department at Santa Clara College, and he was recognized as one of the leading authorities in electrical and chemical science in the world and as an inventor. He died of injuries sustained in an experimental flight in 1911.

Many in Yuba City mourned his death and remembered the Montgomery family fondly, even though they had moved to San Francisco in 1864. John's father, Zach Montgomery, was district attorney for Sutter County in the 1850s and represented this district in the Assembly in 1860. Local citizens remembered that John had designed and worked on his first aircraft before leaving Yuba City. He experimented with plans and crude models in an old shed in the family's backyard on B Street.

RIVER TRANSPORT

In 1850, the steamer *Linda* stopped at

The Yuba City station of the Southern Pacific Railroad was located on Bridge Street east of Shasta Street.

Elements that remain of the Northern Electric railroad bridge bring to mind an era of transportation that might serve us well today. Yuba City residents could conveniently step on a train to travel north to Chico or south to Sacramento or the Bay Area.

Yuba City three days a week. The citizens of Yuba City tried earnestly to promote their city as the terminal point for navigation on the river. Yuba City had an advantage, because the riverbanks were high and accessible year round. Marysville's landing was often submerged at times of high water. However, Yuba City failed to secure a steamboat line.

As agriculture grew in Sutter County, navigation took on an even greater importance than passenger service, as almost all shipping of crops was done by river until about 1890, when railroads took over. A veritable fleet of steamboats plied the waters of the Feather River. Barges were often towed behind the boats to carry the loads of grain.

By 1893, mining debris in the rivers created such hazards to navigation that insurance companies would no longer insure Feather River steamers or their cargoes. Without insurance, the boats could not operate.

After a dozen years, when few steamers came up the river, a renewed hope for the success of navigation came with the arrival of the *Dover* at Yuba City on May 24, 1908. She docked near the Feather River Bridge after a thirteen-and-a-half-hour trip from Sacramento. Her cargo was 300 tons of structural steel for the Great Western Power Company, then installing the lines for the Yuba-Sutter area. The *Dover* made a second trip on June 14, with a 400-ton load of steel, but her crew had to blow snags out of the river to get here. The *Flora* made several trips up the Feather with a barge load of freight, but she had snag troubles near Nicolaus. The *Weitchpec* made weekly trips between Marysville and San Francisco in 1914, but low water and poor river conditions forced her to stop. However, the *Weitchpec* had succeeded in bringing down the price of railroad freight by providing competition, which was the purpose her owners had in mind. It was an end to a colorful, productive era of shipping and navigation on the Feather River.

The steamer *Weitchpec* was built in 1904 to determine if river transport was still viable. In this May 23, 1913 photo, the only person identified is Clarence Wallace on the upper deck next to the flagpole. The *Weitchpec* was destroyed by fire in 1920.

Yuba City MATTERS

Clara Smith photographed the Sutter County Courthouse around 1900. Second Street was unpaved, and posts along the edge of the street offered a place to tie up a horse.

"Yuba City in Year 1881— Looking Back to 'Town by River'"
Independent-Farmer, May 30, 1941

How different Yuba City now appears than it did in 1881! Second Street was a busy thoroughfare, with hotels, saloons and grocery stores.

Then the Yuba City Brewery, with Fred Klempp as proprietor sold No. 1 lager beer for $1.50 for five gallon and $3.00 for ten gallon kegs. The brewery is now occupied by the Neon Sign Co. Across the street on the corner was a grocery store with W. P. Harkey and C. E. Wilcoxon owners. On this corner also there was a well where cold water could be obtained.

Dr. T. H. Ferguson had his office upstairs in the Dobbins building on Bridge Street. Next to this building was the Farmer's Union Bank, with George Ohleyer manager. By the bank was the O. K. Saloon with J. Van Tassell as proprietor. Upstairs over the bank was the office of the newspaper, "The Banner", which was bought by a group of farmers in February of 1881. The name of this paper, under the management of George Ohleyer, was changed to "The Sutter County Farmer". G. W. Alberti, coroner and public administrator, had his office in The Farmer office.

Postoffice Was Where Independent-Farmer Is

In the same block with the brewery on Second Street was the blacksmith shop, owned by Orr and Bunce, and on the opposite side of the street was the Windsor Hotel, with F. Wilbur as proprietor. Then came O. Moncur's office where well boring tools could be obtained.

The postoffice was next to the Windsor Hotel where the Independent-Farmer office is now. Below the postoffice was the general store owned by Jonas Marcuse. The Ernest C. Kimball drug store was located where the Frank Bremer hardware store now stands. Dr. Norman S. Hamlin had his office in this drug store.

Back of the Windsor Hotel and the postoffice on Sutter Street was a large flour mill owned by T. B. Hull. Across the street was the M. E. church.

Farmer's Union Warehouse Stood on River Bank

The home of Judge Phillip Keyser was on the levee at the end of Keyser Street. His house is still there.

There was a large corral where the Masonic Hall now stands. Here the cattle were kept before they were loaded on the boats, which came up the river. All night long one could hear the low of the cattle and the bleat of the sheep.

Just around the corner on B Street was Dr. J. G. Cannon's office. Mrs. Lambert's boarding house was where the Hewitt home now is. Across the street was the I. C. McQuaid home.

Back of the Masonic hall on the levee was a large brick warehouse called the Farmer's Cooperative Union warehouse. There was also a frame warehouse on the site of Dr. Barr's home, which also belonged to the Farmer's Union. The first telephone service in Yuba City was between the Farmer's Union Bank and the brick warehouse. Across the street from this was the Eureka Livery and Sale Stable and Express line, owned by Polk Simmons, who also drove the bus between Marysville and Yuba City. Simmons would stop in front of the houses for his passengers and blow an old fish horn to let the people know he was there.

In 1869, the building at the corner of Second and Bridge streets housed the Masonic Hall upstairs and the Boyd & Wilcoxon Grocery Store below. Left to right are: Ferdinand Klempp, unidentified, Caleb Wilcoxon, M. Strange, Jake Onstott, three unidentified, J. Wilcoxon, unidentified, "Uncle Dickie" Barnett, and Mr. Bickley. One of the next two men is Henry Chism and the other unidentified, as are the remaining two. Note the horse watering trough at the corner.

Parrot in McGee's Stable Swore at Passersby

J. L. Wilbur, attorney-at-law, had his office one door north of the courthouse. McGee's stable stood in this same block next to where the hall of records is. McGee kept a parrot, who always called to anyone passing by and if answered would swear profusely. In the same block was the Yuba City Stable and Express Line with H. Calif as proprietor.

Stabler and Bayne, also attorneys-at-law, had their office opposite the courthouse, in the building now occupied by Judge Hugh D. Moncur.

Dame Kenrod lived on C Street. Across the street was the Sam Kenrod home. The school house was at the end of this street where the Mrs. F. B. Ware home is. The E. Wilcoxon home was at the corner of Second and C Streets. Below the Schillig home were livery stables. Joseph Donovan's blacksmith shop was opposite the Journal office on C Street.

Slough Marked Western Boundary of City Then

At the end of Second Street was the home of Mrs. Mary Raub and Superior Judge J. H. Craddock's home was where Desmond Winship lives.

The frame warehouse was the scene of many of the church bazaars. The booths for these bazaars were very elaborately decorated, the framework being completely covered with flowers, such as violets, roses and poppies, as flowers were plentiful in those days as now.

The slough made the boundaries for the town. On the north side of the town along the levee were some Chinese washhouses and a saloon or two.

Sutter County in 1881 was a prosperous place. The farms were not large as California ranches went in those days, but the average size was about three hundred and twenty acres, with well improved barns and fences and many fine residences. There were good schools and many churches which furnished a large amount of social activities.

The main crop raised on these ranches was grain. One can get an idea of the amount of grain raised by the daily shipments, which amounted to between two hundred and two hundred and fifteen tons daily. This grain was loaded onto steamers, one of which was the D. E. Knight. This steamer also carried the passengers to the picnics that were held at Hock Farm. These picnics were very popular and were well attended by all classes of people.

The Briggs peach orchard was an attraction for people near and far.

YUBA CITY— ONE OF THE BEST COMMUNITIES IN GREAT VALLEY

"Just Across the Feather River From the City of Marysville Two Court Houses are Only a Mile Apart—A Wealthy Section"
Daily Appeal, November 27, 1910

Yuba City, one of the prettiest residence towns in California, is just across the Feather river from Marysville. The river is the corporate limit lines of the two cities. Yuba City has about 2,000 population and Marysville has about 7,000. As a community, so far as churches and fraternal organizations go, they are one city.

Both are county seats of their respective counties, Sutter and Yuba, and in an air line their court houses are only a mile apart.

Yuba City is incorporated in the sixth class and is at the head of navigation on the Feather. Both the Southern Pacific and Northern Electric pass through the city. It also has an excellent street car service connecting it with Marysville. The town has many good streets and suburban driveways, several miles of cement sidewalks, pretty homes with private groves of orange, lemon and other citrus and deciduous trees, well kept lawns and flower gardens. A newly constructed municipal water works system costing over $30,000 gives an abundant supply of water for domestic purposes and affords adequate fire protection. The town is lighted by electricity and there is also an excellent gas and telephone system. The business firms include a bank in a new $40,000 class "A" building, two general merchandise stores, two cigar and confectionery stores, two newspapers and printing offices, two barber shops, two meat markets, a bakery, creamery with ice plant, hardware store, lumber yard, drug store, plumber's shop, ice depot, livery stable, wood yard, flour mill, real estate offices, and other smaller lines of business. There are also four attorneys, three doctors and other professional men.

Near the business part of the town are located the county buildings, which include a two-story court house, and adjoining the same the hall of records, the latter being a stone structure entirely fire proof. These buildings occupy half a block of well kept lawn, on which are planted palm and other tropical trees. Besides these buildings here is a $20,000 Masonic Temple constructed of concrete, a two-story Odd Fellows' building, a public hall, the Woodmen hall in the Bank building, two churches, depots, etc. Plans are being perfected for a new and modern hotel building.

The town, being located in one of the principal fruit growing districts of the state has within its limits two large canneries and one large packing house, which during the season employ from three hundred to five hundred people each. Most of this help consists of women and girls and extra good wages are made. The capacity of the two canneries is four million cans during one season and the packing

Hall of Records, Sutter Co. Yuba City, Cal.

The Sutter County Hall of Records, built in 1891, was originally unpainted, as this circa 1900 photo indicates. Its Romanesque Revival-style and fireproof materials suggest fortress-like security and an air of permanence.

house has an output of over four thousand tons of dried fruit, raisins, almonds, etc., each, while several local shipping firms send out several hundred carloads of fresh and dried fruit. There is also a big fruit drying plant in the town and a large grain warehouse, besides the flour mill and other manufacturing concerns. Yuba City is one of the principal fruit shipping points in the state.

The fraternal societies are well represented, there being a Masonic Lodge, Royal Arch Chapter, Eastern Star Chapter, Odd Fellows and Rebekah Degree Lodge, Encampment, Woodmen of the World Camp, Circle of Woodcraft, all with large memberships. A Woman's Improvement Club is also active and there are other social and business organizations.

Inside a popular cigar store on Second Street are owner Al Walthers at left and Dr. J. G. Cannon. According to Ida Peck Davis, "There were some lively card games that went on beyond the center door in the rear."

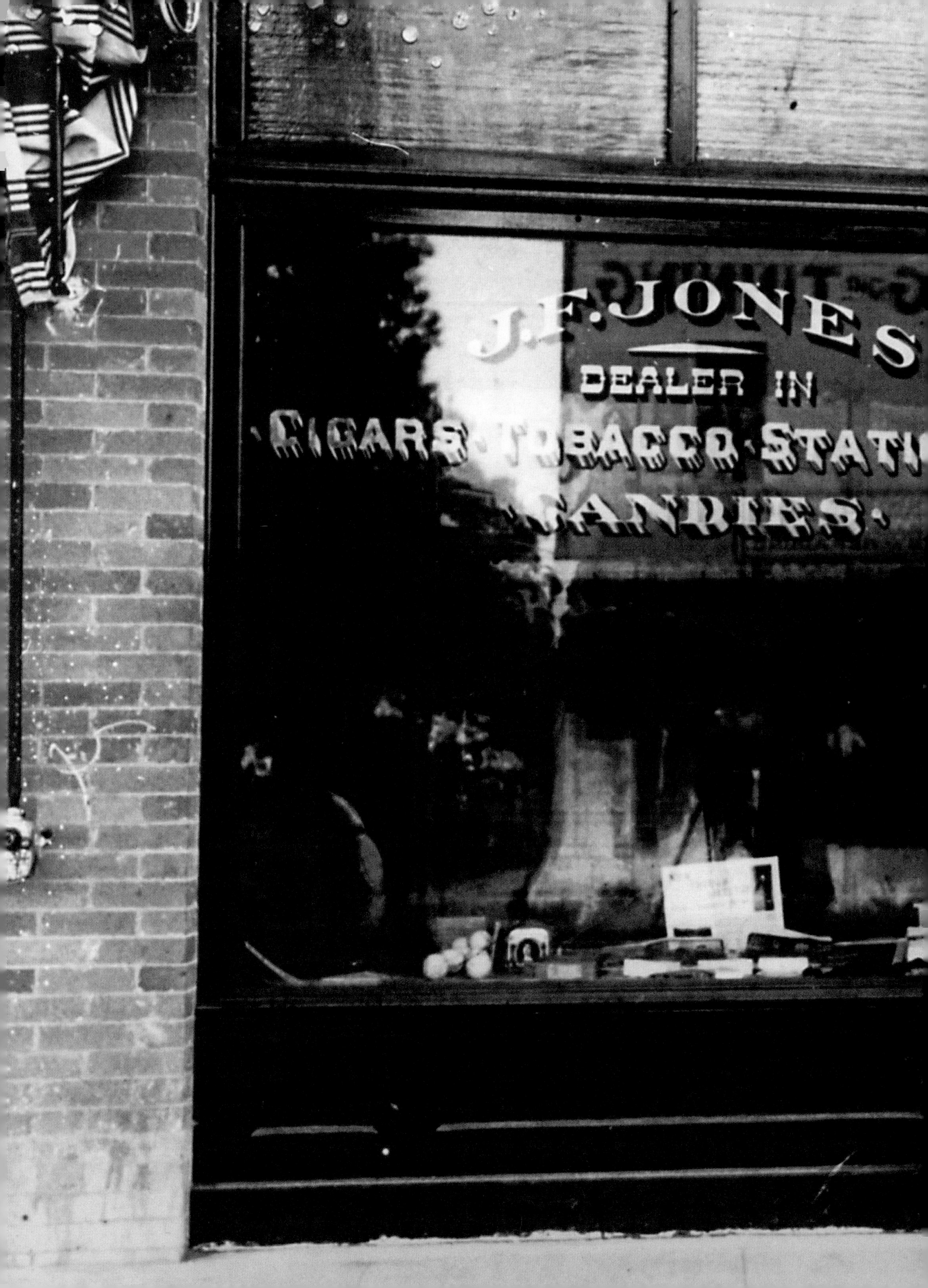
J.F. JONES
DEALER IN
CIGARS TOBACCO STATI
CANDIES.

Jim and Lewis Jones show off their establishment on Second Street between Bridge and Fairman streets in 1907.

Yuba City Newspapers

The first newspapers in Yuba City began publishing in April 1867: the *Weekly Sutter Banner* and the *Sutter County Sentinel*.

The weekly *Sutter County Farmer* began April 22, 1881, and was published for fifty-four years. The *Sutter Independent* joined it in 1886, and the two merged to become the *Independent-Farmer* in 1935.

The weekly *Yuba City Herald* was established in August 1935. On August 5, 1947, the *Independent-Herald* and the *Bi-County Farmer* began publication. The *Independent-Herald* became a daily in 1973, and later became the *Morning Herald* in 1977. The paper ceased publication briefly, and reemerged as the *Valley Herald* until the late 1980s, when the paper closed.

Growth

In May 1930, a preliminary report of the result of the 1930 census indicated Yuba City's population was 3,606, a 111 percent gain over the 1920 census figure of 1708. *The Sutter County Farmer* reported:

The city is fast stepping up into the 4,000 class which will no doubt be reached before the close of the year. According to the report, there are 17 farms within the city, a farm being counted as a tract of land of three acres or over. Yuba City had a population in 1910 of 1,160, in 1920 of 1,708, and in 1930 of 3,606, and more to hear from. The Marysville report gives that city 5,760 at present, 5,461 in 1920 and 5,430 in 1910.

The town of Yuba City also tried to help out citizens who were out of work, money, and food during the Great Depression by offering food in exchange for work cleaning up city properties.

"City Relief Work Proves Successful"
The Sutter County Farmer, March 9, 1933

The relief work conducted by the city council is proving very successful and indications are that the city will keep within the amount of $600 budgeted for this work.

This was the report of Mayor J. H. LePine to the city council on Monday night. In return for the $600 paid out for relief work the city will have its baseball diamond, parks, and other public grounds cleaned of weeds and trash and put in good condition.

So far the city has given out 64 orders for foodstuffs at a cost of 36 cents per order. Mayor LePine estimates that 1,200 orders will be given out before the end of the fiscal year in July.

McRae & Son General Merchandise store featured a display of Hills Brothers Coffee in their window. Signs proclaim "W.O.W. use Hills Brothers Coffee." The large ax symbolized the Woodmen of the World, whose fraternal hall was above the store, circa 1910.

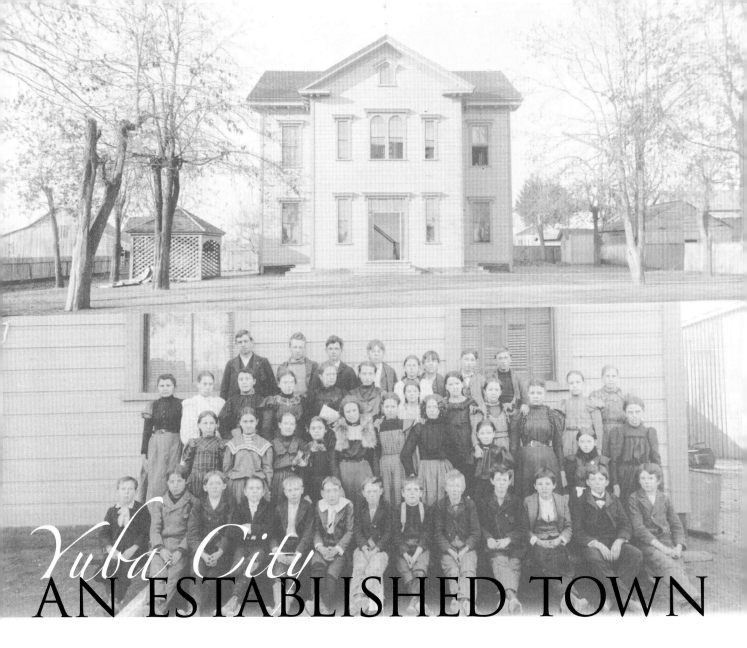

Yuba City
AN ESTABLISHED TOWN

The first elementary school was built in 1856 on what is today the northeast corner of C Street and McRae Way. The first teacher was C. E. Wilcoxon. This 1896 photograph pictures the entire student body and the teacher. This schoolhouse burned in 1900.

SCHOOLS

Looking toward its future, Yuba City examined how to cultivate its most important crop—its children. A census in 1852 shows that there were seventy-five children in Sutter County.

In the spring of 1854, C. E. Wilcoxon pushed for and then taught the first school term in Yuba City. The first term lasted three months and took place in a little clapboard building owned by John Kupser at the corner of C Street and Phipps Alley (later called McRae Way). The elementary school and the newly authorized Masonic Lodge in Yuba City shared this building until 1870, when the Lodge built a new home at the corner of Bridge and Second streets. The clapboard building on C Street was replaced by a two-story schoolhouse, and classes were held there until the construction of a new elementary school, another two-story wooden building at the corner of Bridge and Plumas streets.

In a photograph taken in approximately 1915 from the water tower across the street (see pages 64–65), you can see the new elementary school surrounded by orchards, a packinghouse, unpaved streets, and a few farmhouses. Plumas Street had not yet overtaken Second Street as the commercial hub of the town. This building served the community for many years, but eventually the town outgrew its capacity. For economic reasons, construction of the next school on the Bridge and Plumas street site developed in stages beginning in 1930. Built of brick for fire resistance, the first section consisted of a wing that paralleled Bridge Street. Later, a matching wing along Plumas Street took shape. During this time, the two-story wooden structure still stood. Once both wings were available for classes, the wooden structure was demolished and offices and an auditorium took its place. Two wings of the school were joined to form a corner entrance. The brick school lasted for decades with the beautiful entrance demonstrating the brick mason's skill. A

The Yuba City High School shop class assembles in front of the barn that served as their first classroom in the 1922–1923 school year.

portion of the old brick school remains. At the request of the architect Robert Mackensen, its roof tiles were used when the new school was constructed in 1975.

With the baby boom of the post–World War II years, Yuba City outgrew its only elementary school. Park Avenue School, begun in 1950, consisted of two classrooms, but grew along with the demand for more classroom space. Later, the Gray Avenue, King Avenue, and April Lane schools were constructed to meet the needs of the community.

Green
Marysville

A view from the Yuba City water tower focuses on Yuba City Grammar School at the corner of Bridge and Plumas streets, but also surveys the farmlands and orchards to the south circa 1915.

In 1922, the town constructed the third high school in the county. It looked like the school might come as early as 1892, when Sutter City and Yuba City began competing for the county's first high school. The outlook was good for Yuba City, but a shift in the political winds caused the first high school to be built in Sutter City.

In 1902, revived interest in establishing a high school prompted the creation of a Union District which would include adjacent school districts. These districts would feed students into the high school and financially support it. Once again there was a long hiatus, but interest in a high school in Yuba City grew. Children of high school age in Yuba City attended either Sutter High School or Marysville High School. Yuba County billed Sutter County thousands of dollars to cover the cost of educating those students who attended Marysville High School.

Finally, in August 1922, an overwhelming majority (599 to 42) of citizens in the Yuba City, Lincoln, Barry, Grant, Central, Gaither, and Wilson school districts voted to form the Yuba City Union High School District. The next order of business was to elect a Board of Trustees for the district, and V. W. "Bert" Cooley, Arthur Coats, Carl K. Schnabel, H. C. McMahon, and E. L. Davis filled the Board. The first principal, Cree T. Work, was hired prior to the school opening, and the elementary school found that it could spare three classrooms for the first year of high school operation. R. W. Skinner, Board President Carl Schnabel's father-in-law, purchased three cottages south of the elementary school from B. B. Manford, who had moved them into town from Sutter, and offered them to the district to use as temporary classrooms. The barn on the school grounds was converted for use as a shop class. All of these buildings fronted Plumas Street. The first students began their high school studies in Yuba City on October 2, 1922.

Meanwhile, the search was on to find a permanent home for the high school. What a search it turned out to be! Dr. George H. Jackson offered free land next to the levee near the present-day Sutter County Airport. The school board accepted the gift under certain conditions.

Their primary concern was that a dirt levee at the site be moved and, in a letter addressed to Levee District No. 1, they asked if this could be done. The Levee District refused to move the levee, and the search for a likely site for the high school was renewed.

Originally, five sites were offered for the school. Real estate machinations ensued and offers were made, sweetened, and analyzed. The Board split on its vote and finally decided to turn the matter over to the voters.

In a special election, the options were whittled down to a choice between the Jackson site or the Van Arsdale site. Would the high school be located behind the dirt levee at the free Jackson site, with the understanding that Dr. Jackson would build another levee on his

An aerial view of the original Yuba City High School on B Street reveals its setting amid farmland in the 1930s.

Children sing at a program in front of the Yuba City Grammar School at Bridge and Plumas streets circa 1915.

land, hoping that the dirt levee already present in front of the school would be removed? Or would E. G. Van Arsdale's reduced price for land that already had improvements attract voters? Time was short, but campaigning was vigorous. The most striking campaign feature was a double-page advertisement listing the positives about the Van Arsdale site and the negatives about the Jackson site. The advertisement was signed "The Yuba City Union High School Progressives." Van Arsdale denied any connection to the group and referred questions to L. M. Bunce and F. W. Cooper, leaders of the pro-Van Arsdale site group.

People lined up to vote on Saturday, January 15, 1923, for what was thought to be a tight race. When the counting was finished, the Van Arsdale site won overwhelmingly, 733 to 413.

Funding for the new school came from a $250,000 bond measure. After paying $32,000 for the Van Arsdale property and approving the plans for the school, the Board solicited bids. Much to the Board's surprise, the lowest bid came in at $300,000. Because of time constraints, the Board did not want to have plans resubmitted. They simply crossed out certain parts of the school plan to come in on budget. Construction began in June 1923, with the shop building being the first part of construction. They temporarily divided the shop into four classrooms, as the increasing number of students at the elementary school meant that the high school had to vacate the rooms they used there. On February 4, 1924, students left the temporary buildings behind and moved into their new home. The first graduating class, the Class of 1924, consisted

Construction on Bridge Street School began in 1930. This stylish brick building was demolished in 1975 to make way for the current school.

Yuba · Grammar · School
· Yuba City, Cal ·

Graduating
Exercises ·

Friday Evening, May 24th, 1895.

GEO. W. OGDEN, Principal.

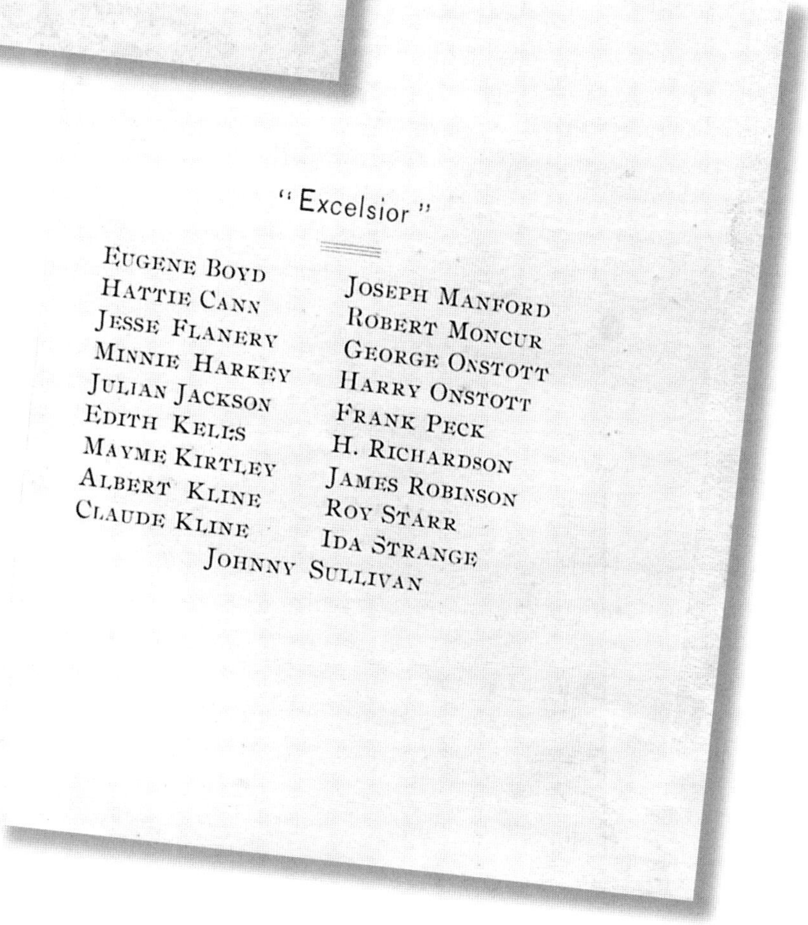

"Excelsior"

EUGENE BOYD
HATTIE CANN
JESSE FLANERY
MINNIE HARKEY
JULIAN JACKSON
EDITH KELLS
MAYME KIRTLEY
ALBERT KLINE
CLAUDE KLINE

JOSEPH MANFORD
ROBERT MONCUR
GEORGE ONSTOTT
HARRY ONSTOTT
FRANK PECK
H. RICHARDSON
JAMES ROBINSON
ROY STARR
IDA STRANGE

JOHNNY SULLIVAN

The entire sophomore class of the school year 1922–1923 poses in front of one of the temporary classroom buildings that were used until the new school was ready for use.

of Thelma Leora Fine and Marjorie Grey Wilcox, with the ceremony held in front of the new high school.

The high school, as a reflection of overall growth in the community, continued to expand. Within two years, the Board of Trustees was asking for an additional $30,000 in order to build the gymnasium that had been deleted because of expense two years earlier. Following decades of growth, building replacement, and temporary classrooms (including Quonset huts from Beale), a second high school, River Valley High School, was opened more than eighty years after the first.

In 1966–1967, the Yuba City Unified School District took shape, and today it includes April Lane, Barry, Bridge Street, Butte Vista, Central Gaither, King Avenue, Lincoln, Lincrest, Park Avenue, Riverbend, Tierra Buena, West Walton, Andros Karperos, Gray Avenue, Albert Powell, River Valley High School, and Yuba City High School. With the growth of our community, it is only a matter of time before Yuba City considers yet another addition to its education roll call.

A small fleet of school buses served the new Yuba City High School in the 1920s. They were manufactured by Fageol, a firm known for their tractors.

In October 1953, teenagers gathered on Plumas Street for a Yuba City High School pep rally for the Big Little Game with Marysville High School.

CHURCHES

Religion has long held influence over life in Yuba City. Complex native religions developed over thousands of years in California, including the area to become Yuba City. From the earliest days of settlement in Yuba City, church services have been held here. Today, there are nearly fifty formal places of worship in Yuba City. The earliest churches here were Christian, but, over the years, other houses of worship have appeared as our population has become more diverse, with three Sikh temples, a Hindu temple, and a mosque offering religious services and guidance in the community.

Formal church services were first held in Yuba City in 1850, when the Methodist Episcopal (M. E.) Church established the Feather River Circuit to serve settlers in Sutter, Yolo, Yuba, and Butte counties. Services were held in homes and in the Western and Elkhorn hotels. Later, the services were held at the courthouse, until the congregation built its church on Yolo Street.

In 1844, a schism in the national M. E. Church occurred over slavery and resulted in the formation of the Methodist Episcopal Church South.

Clara Smith photographed the Methodist Episcopal Church, built in 1872, on Yolo Street between Fairman and Bridge streets, around 1910.

In 1854, followers of the M. E. Church South organized in Yuba City, but their early local records are lost. Eventually they had enough members and the funds to build a church at the corner of C and Second streets. The original church building was replaced in 1921. The building now serves as the county clerk's office.

In 1939, the church schism was mended, and the newly reunited Methodist Episcopal Church held their services at the church at C and Second streets. Plans were made for larger quarters, and in 1951 the church moved to a new home on B Street. Later, the congregation moved yet again to its new home on Colusa Highway.

In 1873, the Baptists, under the pastoral guidance of Pastor Gage, began to hold services. They used the M. E. Church South building for two or three years, but as membership dwindled through death and relocation, and services were discontinued. In 1924, the First Baptist Church of Yuba City began meeting in a building that was brought from Richvale for that purpose. Since then, the First Baptist Church has moved into ever larger quarters in the city.

The First Lutheran Church in Yuba City dates back to 1927, when members first met in the Marysville Hall to discuss organizing the church. In 1934, church construction began at 850 Cooper Avenue, with members doing much of the construction. Materials and furnishings included pews that came from the West Butte Community Church. The new church was dedicated in 1935.

Many Christian denominations established churches here in the 1920s and 1930s, including the Assembly of God, Church of Christ, Seventh-Day Adventist, First Church of Christ, Scientist, and First Church of the Nazarene. The Church of Jesus Christ of Latter-Day Saints erected their first church in town in 1949.

The Methodist Episcopal Church at the corner of Second and C streets was photographed from the top of the Sutter County Courthouse around 1939–1940 to record the high waters of the Feather River behind it.

The Methodist Episcopal Church South was on the southwest corner of Second and C streets, circa 1910. The Southern Church later reunited with the Methodist Episcopal Church, and they met in the second church building on this site, built in 1921.

Churchgoers visit after the service at the Lutheran Church at Cooper Street and Forbes Avenue in the 1950s.

St. Isidore's Catholic Church organized in 1952–1953, when an unused chapel from Beale was relocated to Cooper Avenue, and services were led by Marysville priests. In 1953, this building was moved to the Clark Avenue site, and a grammar school, then called Holy Angels, was built. Construction of the present-day church and remodeling of the former chapel into a parish house and youth center followed in 1960.

The first Sikh gurdwara opened in Yuba City in 1969 and has been followed by two other gurdwaras as the Sikh population has grown. The first mosque in Yuba City, The Islamic Center of Yuba City, was destroyed by an arson fire in 1994 just before its completion. Since then, the mosque has been rebuilt and serves its followers. The Sri Narayan Hindu Temple, completed in 1996, serves the local Hindu population.

Church, gurdwara, temple, mosque—they all serve the spiritual needs of Yuba City.

SERVICES

Along with schools and churches, civil services such as medical, fire, and police protection, as well as a city hall, demonstrate the maturation of the town of Yuba City.

The first Sikh temple, or gurdwara, was built on Tierra Buena Road west of Yuba City. Its jewel-like colors and architecture stand out boldly on this rural road. Visitors are always welcome at the gurdwara.

The Church of Jesus Christ of Latter-Day Saints at
Clark Avenue and B Street was built in 1949.

In order to meet the needs of the local Muslim
community, a solemn, beautiful mosque was
erected to the north of the Sikh gurdwara on
Tierra Buena Road.

St. Isidore's Catholic Church and School is located on Clark Avenue.

Although many local immigrants from India and Pakistan are of the Sikh faith, a number follow the teachings of Hinduism. Their stately temple is remarkable in the rural landscape of Franklin Road west of South Walton Avenue.

The City Hall building at 441 Colusa Avenue, then called Sumner Street, was built in 1939. Yuba City received a grant loan from the federal Public Works Administration to build it. It also housed the fire department and police department. When the city moved its offices to Civic Center Boulevard in 1981, this structure was restored for professional offices.

The Yuba City Hospital was located on Plumas Street near Colusa Avenue in the 1920s.

The Sutter County Hospital was built on Live Oak Boulevard, shown below in this 1918 view.

Yuba City
FACING CHALLENGES

In the past 150 years, the residents of Yuba City have faced numerous challenges, some so severe as to impact the entire population and others minor enough to raise a smile. Let's start with some of the events that have impacted the community as a whole.

FLOODS

The threat of flooding during the winter months has always been present in Yuba City. Interest in the history of flooding skyrocketed after the 1955 flood, and an article by Noel Stevenson appeared in the Sutter County Historical Society *Bulletin* in January 1956, which chronicled flooding in the community through the nineteenth century.

The first flood to affect the city occurred in the winter of 1852–1853. By the time of the flood's peak in March 1853, the region was flooded, and travel and communication was done via boat. Farmers moved their stock to high ground, and merchants ran their businesses from the second floor of their buildings. The only recorded dry spot in Yuba City was the Indian rancheria located in the area of Second and C streets.

This photo taken from the top of the Sutter County Courthouse looks at the high water in the Feather River in the late 1930s. Buildings across the street include Mission Hall and the Masonic Hall to the north.

The town—indeed, nearly the entire county—flooded once again in 1861. A vivid description published in the *Marysville Appeal* in December 1861 revealed that "westward one vast water level stretched to Yuba City, where a kindred inundation was raging, the entire town site being under water. Beyond this to the foothills of the coast range there appeared to be no dry land."

The California Legislature established Swamp Land District No. 1, which included Yuba City, in 1866. This was the first state-authorized levee district in California and later was renamed Levee District No. 1.

The levees in both Yuba City and Marysville broke in January 1875, when heavy rain caused the Feather River to rise suddenly. In the *Sacramento Union* it was reported that "the breaks in the levee above Yuba City made two channels through the nursery of Dr. Teegarden causing great havoc and carrying off many trees. The channel of the lowest break is still cutting toward the old Webb house, also owned by Dr. Teegarden, and it is feared that it will be undermined. . . . The north and south walls of the Yuba City courthouse continue to settle, and it is thought that it will suffer material damage." Many blamed the severity of the flooding on the hydraulic mining tailings, and this added impetus to the Anti-Debris Movement.

In mid-March of 1907, the river rose rapidly, and levees broke on both the Marysville and Yuba City sides of the river. In this flood, it was not the amount of water that caused the problem, but the debris clogging the river that caused breaks along a 200-mile expanse. There were multiple breaks south of Yuba City, including one at Starr Bend, which resulted in extensive flooding in Yuba City, with two feet of water on Shasta Street. There was also a break at the Spangler ranch at Shanghai Bend, which contributed to the flooding.

Yuba City managed to stay dry until 1955, when record water flow in the local rivers from a warm December storm, sometimes referred to as the "Pineapple Express," caused the snow pack to melt, while at the same time dropping a great deal of water into the valley. Due to the threat of flooding, Marysville was evacuated, with many residents staying with friends and family in Yuba City. Both civilian and military men from Beale worked furiously on the levees in the area, filling and placing sandbags. Ultimately, the levee gave way at what is referred to as the Gum Tree break at Shanghai Bend, located at Garden Highway and Lincoln Road. Thirty-seven people died in the flood, 40,000 evacuated Yuba City and the surrounding area, and 4,500 homes were flooded. Although there has been periodic flooding in the region, Yuba City has remained dry since 1955.

The town was evacuated in 1997, when high water once again threatened the levee system, but the danger passed in a few days, and

This definitive aerial photo from the December 1955 flood illuminates the Shanghai Bend break in the levee in the upper center and the Fifth Street Bridge with the central portion swept away in the lower left.

The destructive power of the raging water leaves chaos in its wake with only pieces remaining of the railroad bridge and the Fifth Street Bridge.

The dangerous rescue of Norma Bartlett and her infant son from the top of their rapidly submerging auto engaged readers all over the country when photos of the successful rescue appeared in *Life* magazine. Rapidly moving waters overtook the car just under a set of power lines. This was only one of the heartrending human dramas that took place during the December 1955 flood in Yuba City.

evacuees were allowed to return to their homes. We know through experience and history that to live in Yuba City is to remain ever vigilant during periods of high water.

A Killer in Our Midst

In what became known as the crime of the century, labor contractor Juan Corona was arrested, charged, tried twice, and convicted both times for the murders of twenty-five farm workers. Their bodies were found buried in a peach orchard near Yuba City in May 1971. Corona remains in Corcoran State Prison.

Songs Cut Short

The May 21, 1976 bus crash off Interstate 680 in Martinez, which took the lives of twenty-eight Yuba City High School Choir members and one teacher, shook the area and the nation as well. Cards and letters from all over the nation arrived offering condolences and contributions.

Tom Pfeffer, the Yuba City mayor, expressed the community's devastation, saying, "The loss of our High School students has reached into the lives of all the people in our area."

A photographer in a passing boat caught this boat headed north on Plumas Street, December 1955. The Christmas decorations over the flooded street lend poignancy to the scene.

In May 1979, City Council representatives from Yuba City presented a plaque to the City Council of the city of Martinez in appreciation of the kindness and compassion shown by the city following the bus crash. In 1988, twenty-eight Bishop pines were planted at the Martinez Regional Shoreline. A bench and wooden plaque with the names of the Yuba City High School students who died in the accident were included as a memorial. A plaque marks the loss at Yuba City High School as well.

Not all of our challenges have been nearly as devastating. In the late nineteenth century, Yuba City found itself unable to quench its thirst.

The U.S. Post Office patrons would have had to row in during the December 1955 flood when Plumas Street looked more like a river than the main business district.

A house on Percy Avenue was tossed onto the railroad tracks by the 1955 floodwaters and left high and dry there when the waters receded.

PROHIBITION

One of the earliest businesses in Yuba City was the Bottler Brothers Brewery, built around 1857 on the riverbank. Due to high water, it was moved in 1864 to the southeast corner of Second and Bridge streets, where the two-story portion remains today.

Frederick Klempp, a native of Germany, became manager of the brewery in 1879, and, under his guidance, the business expanded to include a saloon adjacent to the brewery.

In a not entirely popular move, Sutter County Supervisors approved a prohibition ordinance in October 1891, outlawing the sale or giving away of intoxicating beverages. Fortunately for those who enjoyed spirits now and then, the enterprising Klempp opened the "Cliff House" bar, sometimes called "Last Chance Saloon," just on the other end of the covered bridge on the Marysville side. Naturally a popular establishment, it provided an opportunity for a last drink before entering the "dry" territory of Sutter County. Mrs. May Louise Baker remembered that, despite Yuba City being "dry," men could get their jugs filled for their own consumption at the brewery.

In the September 25, 1892 *Daily Appeal* is a report of the "silver-tongued temperance orator Francis Murphy" speaking at Turner Hall in Marysville with the result that thirty persons, mostly men, signed temperance pledges. Murphy's appearance is indicative of the strong sweep of the temperance movement throughout the country in this era.

Prohibition was debated in Sutter County throughout the next few decades, as many businessmen felt that it seriously limited Yuba City's potential for commercial growth.

Yuba City fell under the prohibition ordinance of Sutter County, and, consequently, inhabitants complied with the Volstead Act at a higher level than their counterparts on the Marysville side. That is not to say that one could not get a drink in Yuba City. In the Sutter County Historical Society *Bulletin*, Eugene Gray remembered only a few places in Sutter County where liquor was sold, but the Cotton Club stood out in his memory with its "palms and lush and beautiful vegetation, it provided a place to dine, dance and drink for the discriminating." In 1920, the owner of the Hotel Sutter on Bridge Street was charged with selling liquor. In Marysville, it seemed one could buy a drink almost anyplace. Mr. Gray observed that one of the most popular clubs was located right across the street from the police station.

It was not only on the east bank of the Feather River that liquor laws were ignored. Some creative entrepreneurs went right down the river with their illegal business. Called "blind piggers," these "booze steamers" plied their business on the Feather River.

Although Sutter County had a prohibition ordinance for nearly forty years,

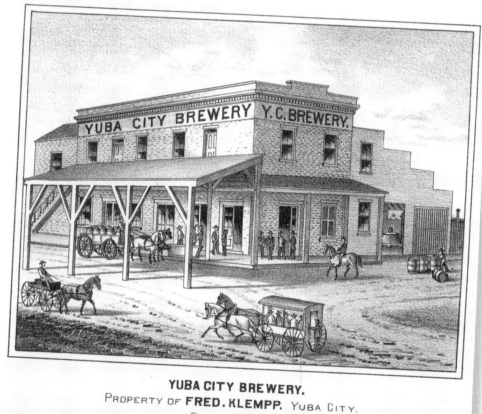

YUBA CITY BREWERY.
PROPERTY OF **FRED. KLEMPP.** YUBA CITY.
SUTTER CO. CAL.

Illustration from Thompson & West's *History of Sutter County*, published in 1879.

The Cliff House Yuba City Brewery Beer Depot was
located on the Marysville side of the Feather River near
the covered bridge, convenient for a last drink before
crossing into dry Yuba City and Sutter County. This
esteemed structure was swept away in the 1907 flood.

In 1930, the California National Guard Armory on B Street appeared much the same as it does today.

The Sutter County Farmer reported that "Sutter County Votes Wet By 2 to 1 as Dry Law is Voided" in the election of November 1932. It had been a long dry spell, soon to end, as the 18th Amendment would be repealed on December 5, 1933.

Criminal acts and unwanted visitors are always irritating, but some of them recorded in local papers revealed daring, imagination, and a sense of humor.

Boy Scouts collect aluminum for a World War II defense drive.

Highway Men

On October 8, 1908, the *Daily Appeal* reported that M. J. Miller, a painter, and his wife were held up on Teegarden Avenue, a seldom-used lane, by two highwaymen, who sprang out in front of the horse with guns pointed. Miller put his hand down as if to reach for a gun, and the two backed up. He then gave his horse the whip and sped off. The holdup occurred near the bridge over the slough on Teegarden.

Van Arsdale's Store

The Sutter County Farmer reported on February 2, 1900, that E. G. Van Arsdale's store was broken into by burglars in the night. They took several watches and gold-plated chains and the seven dollars contained in the cash register. The villains took time "to suck five or six eggs from the basket in the rear of the store and threw the shells around on the floor."

Judge Shields of Sacramento dedicated the Veterans' Park at Second and Bridge streets on May 30, 1922. James H. Barr raised the flag. The park honored the eleven area war dead of World War I, and a tree was planted to honor each fallen soldier. Veterans' Park has recently been restored.

"Thief Leaves Note Thanking for Loot"
The Marysville Appeal, November 22, 1922

Adding insult to injury is the burglar who steals your belongings and then leaves a note thanking you for the appropriated gifts.

It was enough to have some sneak thief clean out the bean growers and peach growers office on B street last Saturday night; and it was too much that that person should leave the polite acknowledgement of "thanks for the typewriter, signed 'Bum' and 'Nut'". The note was found today.

"Thief Looks Up Law On 'Burglary' While In Hewitt's Office"
The Marysville Appeal, November 28, 1922

Entering the office of Attorney A. H. Hewitt on Second street, by way of a rear window, Saturday or Sunday night, a burglar ransacked all parts of the room, tore up documents, peered into law books and finally departed, taking with him a stamp affixer containing about $8 in stamps and a check protector.

From all appearances the burglary was committed by the same party who last week entered the office of the California Bean Growers association and took an electric fan and a typewriter.

Before leaving Hewitt's office the intruder pasted two stamps on the door and scattered rubber bands from one part of the room to the other. Undersheriff Shelly who investigated the case states that a law book was found opened to a section pertaining to "burglary" and that apparently the penalties prescribed therein caused the thief to make a hasty retreat, taking the loot with him however.

Unwelcome Visitors

"Ku Klux Klan In Yuba City—Robed Klansmen Attend Church Services On Court House Lawn, Visit Dying Resident of This Place"
The Sutter County Farmer, August 11, 1922

Yuba City has a Ku Klux Klan. The Knights of this Invisible Empire have made their initial appearance in this county, attended church services on the court house lawn, and visited a resident of this place who was dying. Garbed in their mysterious robes with masks over their faces, six Klansmen marched solemnly down the aisle through the congregation of the local church here when services were being held on the court house lawn last Sunday evening, the leader taking his place before the meeting and holding up his hand interrupted the services long enough to read a short message after which they marched to the street and entering a closed automobile drove away. No one recognized any of the klan. . . .

It has been reported for some time that the Ku Klux Klan were getting ready to organize in Yuba and Sutter counties, but this is the first appearance of the Klan. It is presumed that their activities will be confined to peaceful demonstrations and under such circumstances no objections will be made to their organizing. If, however, there is any interference on their part with the rights of others or any acts of violence or disturbing of the peace, the officers of the town and county will step in.

District Attorney Arthur Coats had authorized this announcement from his office: "I believe that Ku Klux Klan is inimical to good government and I deplore their arrival in Sutter County. So far as it lies in my power I will oppose, with every means the law affords me, any attempt of any organization to take the law into its own hands and out of the hands of the constituted authorities."

WEATHER

Everyone knows that we are blessed with a pleasant climate. Once in a long while, there can be departures from the norm. In December 1932, Yuba City experienced a record-breaking cold spell with a low of 11 degrees and the thermometer lingering in the teens for over a week. Citrus trees were killed, making it evident that oranges could not be grown commercially here. Even deciduous trees sustained damage. Packing plants and other businesses were forced to shut down, schools closed, countless homes suffered burst water pipes, and automobiles were damaged. The nearest to this record had been in 1888, when a low of 18 degrees was recorded.

NATIONAL SERVICE

Included in the city's challenges are the times when residents have left home to fight for our freedoms. Those left behind waited for their loved ones to return and showed their respect for those lost and those welcomed home.

CITY NO. 329

Lastly, our community faced a challenge when rated at the very bottom of Rand-McNally's 1985 *Places Rated Almanac: Your Guide to Finding the Best Places to Live in America*. Mayor Chuck Pappageorge responded, "If we'd been second to last, no one would have noticed. This is a great opportunity. We'll get some yardage out of it." The

RAND-McNALLY KISS YOUR ATLAS!
FROM THE GOOD FOLKS OF YUBA-SUTTER

dubious distinction and consequent notoriety was widely publicized in *Life, Time,* and *People* magazines. A "329 Committee" was set in motion to capitalize on it.

Representative Gene Chappie defended Yuba City on the House Floor stating that Yuba City "is not a city at all. It is a safe, clean and sunny little farm community and it intends to stay that way." Supporters wrote poems and odes to Yuba City, and 90 Proof Country recorded the song "I'd Rather Live in Yuba City" with lyrics by Austin Lewis.

The Veterans' Memorial in front of the Veterans' Hall on Butte House Road is an eloquent tribute to all the veterans from Sutter County.

MASONIC HALL,
YUBA CITY, CALIF.

Yuba City
SOCIAL LIFE

The Masonic Hall on the northeast corner of Second and B streets was built in 1907 and is still in use by Enterprise Masonic Lodge.

In the early years of Yuba City, people joined fraternal lodges, not only for social interaction, but to provide what might be called an early form of insurance. In case of illness or death, the lodge would provide assistance to the member or to the widow or orphans of the member. Lodges also performed important civic improvement work.

Enterprise Lodge No. 70, Free & Accepted Masons was the first lodge established in Yuba City in 1855. The Independent Order of Odd Fellows was chartered in 1871. Yuba City Grange No. 65 was organized in 1873 to work for the betterment of ordinary farmers.

Community service clubs have historically included Kiwanis, Lions, and Rotary groups. Today, there are many service and civic groups active in Yuba City, but community involvement has been a tradition in our hometown since the beginning.

WOMEN'S GROUPS

At the turn of the twentieth century, women primarily worked in the home to care for their families. But a new consciousness was on the horizon for women, with some taking active roles in movements for temperance and suffrage. About this time, women began to organize women's clubs. These served not only as social clubs, but as vehicles for civic and social change.

The first women's club formed in the Yuba City area was Bogue Country Club in 1906. They raised a building fund and built a clubhouse in 1909. The clubhouse at Bogue Road and South Walton Avenue has been demolished, but the club itself, with a dwindling membership, continues.

Another early club was the Yuba City Ladies Improvement Club, formed in 1908. This dynamic group of women built Mission Hall in 1909, a community building across the street from the courthouse. They turned Mission Hall over to Sutter County in 1912 for the sum of fifteen dollars, and it was used for various county offices. The Sutter County Library was located there from 1917 to 1933. Mission Hall was razed in 1954 to make way for the present Sutter County office building.

Tierra Buena Improvement Club was founded in 1913. It was active in civic and community affairs over the years, but recently dissolved.

The Yuba City Women's Club formed in 1924. They got busy right away with civic improvements. In 1927, one of their concerns was what should be done about Yuba City High School students speeding on B Street. They built a clubhouse in 1931 at Plumas Street and Colusa Avenue and contributed to the area in many ways. With their building now sold, the remaining members continue to support the community.

Also active in our community are Soroptimist International of Marysville-Yuba City, founded in 1929, and the American Association of University Women, beginning in 1928.

Of several self-improvement groups, the oldest active literary group is Fortnightly, which celebrated its one hundredth anniversary in 2004. Minutes from the early years stipulated that they were "never to discuss dress, disease or domestics." The Seminar was founded in 1931, and the Literary Guild was established in 1933 and disbanded in 2008.

DANCING

Dancing was enjoyed from the beginning. As early as the 1860s, there are reports of dances held in private homes, schoolhouses, or in the outdoors. In 1874, the Calico Ball took place at Schuessler's Hall, and music was provided by Siebert's Brass and String Band. The Yuba

Members of the Bogue Country Club gather in front of their new clubhouse at the corner of Bogue Road and South Walton Avenue, circa 1910.

City String Band played at a dance at the Farmers' Warehouse on the riverfront in 1876.

The Pacific Brass Band played for a dance in Littlejohn's new barn in 1880. The location was near Franklin Road and Highway 99, where the 1899 Littlejohn home stands today.

Dance venues in Yuba City included the Masonic Hall, the Farmers' Warehouse, Mission Hall, and Yuba City Women's Club. The Peach Pavilion was a popular place on Bridge Street. Nelson's Ballroom, located west of Yuba City, was an L-shaped converted barracks. With the band situated in the corner of the "L," dancers in both wings could hear the music. The Moon Dance Hall was located on the southeast corner of Highway 20 and Acacia, near Sutter, a favorite destination for Yuba City dancers. In Sutter, the Wintergarden Dance Hall on California Street hosted dances. In the Sutter County Historical Society *Bulletin*, Myrtle Newcomb remembered dancing on the floating pavilion of the "Feather

River Resort," which was reached by a gangplank from the Marysville side. Open-air dance pavilions, hastily built, accommodated dancing in several places.

Don Burtis remembers that some local bands were the Rollin Banta Band, the Joe Matthews Band, and Squee Phillips & His Midnight Band. There was also Louis Tyler's Band, Dick McCaffrey's Band, Norman Tyler, George Nakao, Madge Maynard, and the Veltones. Glenn Gauche's Band (1945–1948) evolved into the Don Burtis Orchestra (1948–1958) when Glenn handed it over to Don. Dance clubs were formed, such as the Franklin Dance Club and the Monday Night Dance Club.

During the 1920s and 1930s, a new form of entertainment entered the American scene: marathon dancing. The Yuba City Marathon Dance in 1929 aimed to break the existing state amateur marathon record of 365 hours. Large crowds flocked to the Peach Pavilion to see the couples compete for a $1,000 prize. One couple in the contest was married at the dance, while they, their attendants, and even the officiating judge

Picnickers traveled up the Feather River by barge to the Hook-um Cow dance platform near the Oregon Railroad trestle north of Yuba City in the 1920s.

A crowd gathers for the dedication of the Hock Farm marker on February 8, 1930.

kept dancing. The dance ran continuously for 371 hours before it went terribly awry. In a scandal that shocked Yuba City, the promoters could not pay employees, the Six Red Devils Orchestra, nor the dancers, and they were subsequently arrested and jailed, but let off with a small fine.

YOUTH CLUBS

In the past, few organized clubs for children existed. Boy Scouting came to Yuba City in 1924, when the Buttes Area Council was formed. During the years of World War II, membership reached 898 boys. The Boy Scouts performed over 6,000 hours of service during the local floods of 1950 and 1955.

There were Camp Fire Girl groups as early as 1913. Both the Boy Scouts and the Camp Fire Girls used the Scouts' summer camp at Strawberry Valley. In the 1930s, Camp Fire Girls sold doughnuts instead of candy as their annual fundraising campaign, and they received doughnut-shaped awards to put on their ceremonial gowns.

Picnics were a popular pastime, with favorite destinations in the Sutter Buttes, at John Sutter's Hock Farm, or in several nearby picnic grounds, such as Dow Grove.

When Sutter resided at Hock Farm, he was ever the congenial host, welcoming visitors and feeding them lavishly from the bounty of his ranch and vineyard. Later, the grounds of Hock Farm still attracted picnickers. Often steamboats, with whistles blowing, would bring a packed boatload of celebrants down the river to spend the day enjoying the beautiful grounds. Special occasion gatherings, such as Fourth of July picnics, were held at Hock Farm. In 1875, the fraternal Red Men's Ball took place there. The Marysville Brass Band and String Band provided the music. The steamboat *Yuba City Belle* pulled a barge, filled with dancers, behind it all the way to Hock Farm.

NATION'S CENTENNIAL

The centennial observance of our country's founding was celebrated in 1876 with a big picnic at Hock Farm. The steamboat *D. E. Knight* departed from the Yuba City landing at Farmers' Warehouse packed with picnickers. On the grounds was a stand seating twenty-seven ladies dressed in red, white, and blue, representing the different states, and, in the top seat, Miss Emma Wilcoxon representing the Goddess of Liberty. Judge Keyser gave an historical sketch of Sutter County, and after music and a reading of the Declaration of Independence, Richard Bayne delivered an eloquent oration. There followed an ample picnic dinner and dancing to the Marysville String Band. The steamboat returned home in time for the ball at the Farmers' Warehouse, with music by J. A. Apperson.

Peach
Day
Program

YUBA CITY
SUTTER COUNTY
CALIFORNIA

SATURDAY, JUNE 3
NINETEEN TWENTY-TWO

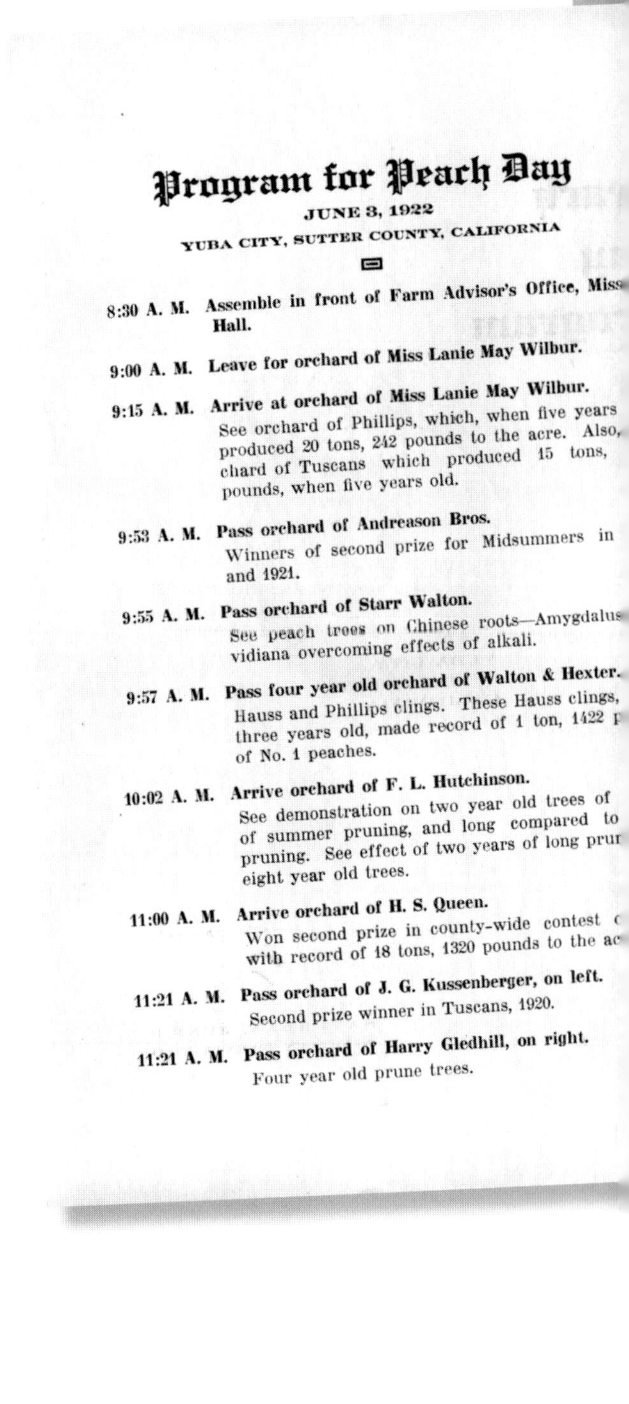

Program for Peach Day
JUNE 3, 1922
YUBA CITY, SUTTER COUNTY, CALIFORNIA

8:30 A. M. Assemble in front of Farm Advisor's Office, Miss
Hall.

9:00 A. M. Leave for orchard of Miss Lanie May Wilbur.

9:15 A. M. Arrive at orchard of Miss Lanie May Wilbur.
See orchard of Phillips, which, when five years
produced 20 tons, 242 pounds to the acre. Also,
chard of Tuscans which produced 15 tons,
pounds, when five years old.

9:53 A. M. Pass orchard of Andreason Bros.
Winners of second prize for Midsummers in
and 1921.

9:55 A. M. Pass orchard of Starr Walton.
See peach trees on Chinese roots—Amygdalus
vidiana overcoming effects of alkali.

9:57 A. M. Pass four year old orchard of Walton & Hexter.
Hauss and Phillips clings. These Hauss clings,
three years old, made record of 1 ton, 1422 p
of No. 1 peaches.

10:02 A. M. Arrive orchard of F. L. Hutchinson.
See demonstration on two year old trees of
of summer pruning, and long compared to
pruning. See effect of two years of long prur
eight year old trees.

11:00 A. M. Arrive orchard of H. S. Queen.
Won second prize in county-wide contest c
with record of 18 tons, 1320 pounds to the ac

11:21 A. M. Pass orchard of J. G. Kussenberger, on left.
Second prize winner in Tuscans, 1920.

11:21 A. M. Pass orchard of Harry Gledhill, on right.
Four year old prune trees.

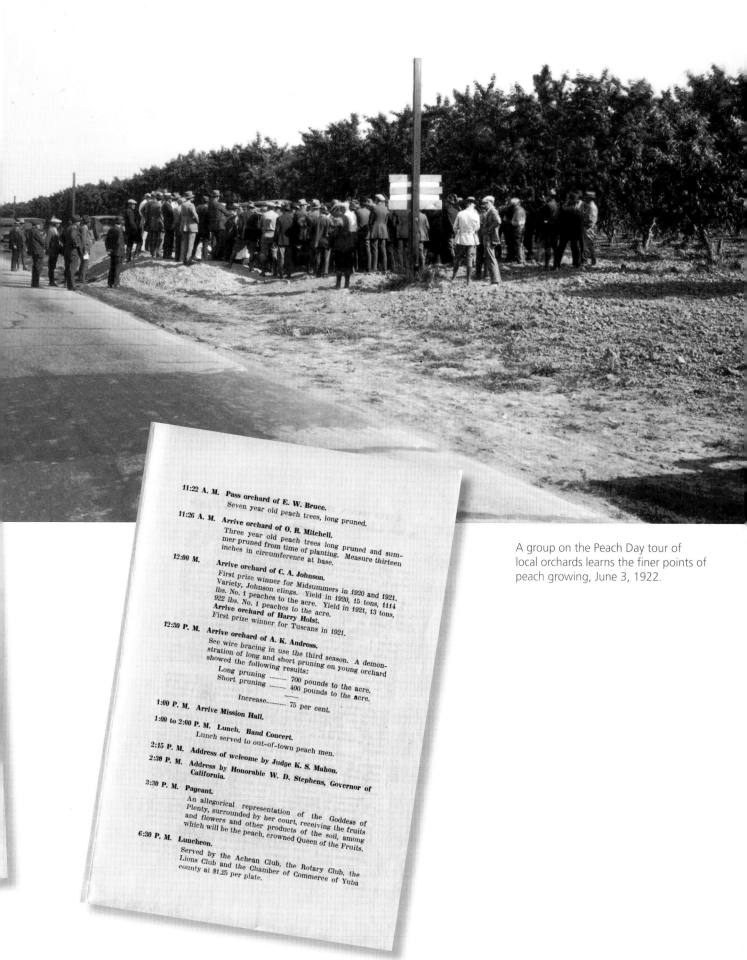

11:22 A. M. **Pass orchard of E. W. Bruce.**
Seven year old peach trees, long pruned.

11:26 A. M. **Arrive orchard of O. R. Mitchell.**
Three year old peach trees long pruned and summer pruned from time of planting. Measure thirteen inches in circumference at base.

12:00 M. **Arrive orchard of C. A. Johnson.**
First prize winner for Midsummers in 1920 and 1921. Variety, Johnson clings. Yield in 1920, 15 tons, 1114 lbs. No. 1 peaches to the acre. Yield in 1921, 13 tons, 922 lbs. No. 1 peaches to the acre.
Arrive orchard of Harry Holst.
First prize winner for Tuscans in 1921.

12:30 P. M. **Arrive orchard of A. K. Andross.**
See wire bracing in use the third season. A demonstration of long and short pruning on young orchard showed the following results:
Long pruning ———— 700 pounds to the acre.
Short pruning ———— 400 pounds to the acre.

Increase............ 75 per cent.

1:00 P. M. **Arrive Mission Hall.**

1:00 to 2:00 P. M. **Lunch. Band Concert.**
Lunch served to out-of-town peach men.

2:15 P. M. **Address of welcome by Judge K. S. Mahon.**

2:30 P. M. **Address by Honorable W. D. Stephens, Governor of California.**

3:30 P. M. **Pageant.**
An allegorical representation of the Goddess of Plenty, surrounded by her court, receiving the fruits and flowers and other products of the soil, among which will be the peach, crowned Queen of the Fruits.

6:30 P. M. **Luncheon.**
Served by the Achean Club, the Rotary Club, the Lions Club and the Chamber of Commerce of Yuba county at $1.25 per plate.

A group on the Peach Day tour of local orchards learns the finer points of peach growing, June 3, 1922.

CELEBRATIONS

Several outstanding celebrations were Peach Day, beginning in 1922, and the Trails of '49 in 1930, a bi-county effort. Smaller events like Booster Week to promote business on Plumas Street, and the National Recovery Act parade and celebration during the Depression, were really extravaganzas. This stellar history of celebration was brought right up into modern times with the California Prune Festival and the various fine events currently sponsored by the city of Yuba City, both promotional and cultural.

"King Whiskerino" Wayne Walkup has a firm hold on the Golden Jubilee Queen Sandy (Mrs. Obie) Wickersham, on the left, and Miss California, Sandra Lee Jennings of Riverside, on the right. The Queen and King were crowned at the grand ball at the fairgrounds, as part of the fiftieth anniversary celebration of Yuba City's incorporation in 1908.

SUTTER COUNTY PEACH DAY

The first Sutter County Peach Day took place on June 3, 1922. Our area was beginning to earn its reputation as "Peach Bowl of the World," so Peach Day was planned by the Farm Bureau as an educational seminar for orchardists from all over the state. The California governor himself, William D. Stephens, said, "I have never seen a get-together of this character with as much pep."

The public relations arm of this event consisted of ten young ladies chosen by the Marysville Lions Club to present peaches to the visitors. The Peach Girls, as they were called, wore peach-colored dresses with peach-shaped pockets, and they posed in peach orchards to promote the Sutter County peach. The Peach Girls were: Beatrice Veckley, Virginia Bruce, Eleanor Dam, Roselind Reed, Betha Bowen, Marhnelle Coats, Vivian Wilcox, Marjorie Smith, Dorothy Seawell, and Alice Hauck.

The first event of Peach Day was an automobile tour of area peach orchards, starting from Mission Hall at 9:00 a.m. The tour was followed by a luncheon at the Masonic Hall, at which Governor Stephens was present.

In 1910, the Odd Fellows Hall at Second and Fairman streets housed businesses on the ground floor, as it does today. These included the *Sutter Independent* newspaper and the People's Meat Market. A gent studies a poster for the upcoming Bachelors' Ball.

At 3:30, on the lawn of the courthouse, a Peach Pageant illustrated Sutter County's riches in agriculture and horticulture. Miss Ruth Harter portrayed the Goddess of Plenty, and Miss Grace Raub, the Peach Queen. The various agricultural products were portrayed by Estelle Brockman and Muriel Walton as grain; Betty Schillig and Dorothy Morley as flowers; Barbara Wilbur and Jean Schillig as grapes; Barbara Walton and Mona Ashley as citrus fruits; B. Brust and M. Lydon as prunes; and A. Lang and A. Woodworth as cherries. Attendants to the Goddess and Queen were Louise Kimball, Bobbie Roberts, Dorothy Scofield, Dorothy Bremer, H. Pierman, Elva Burns, Jane Coats, Harriet Thomas, Marion Hurd, Mina Williamson, June Robinson, and Doris Hill.

In the evening, a banquet featured a speech by the guest of honor, Governor Stephens. The governor praised the Peach Day celebration, the area's peach production, and the cooperative marketing associations. Madge Maynard's Orchestra provided the music. The evening ended with a street dance in Yuba City to the tunes of Wagner's Orchestra. The grand finale was a magnificent display of fireworks, ending an unprecedented celebration.

Winners of a silver cup for their rifle team, the Yuba City Woodmen of the World pose in 1917. Pictured in the back row, left to right, are Ben Manford, Clive Kelly Ling, O. Gamuon, Ben Schillig, Bob Taylor, and D. Mount. Pictured in the front row, left to right, are Mr. Stone, Tim Plant, Al Onstott, George Ohleyer, Jr., and Orlin Wallace.

TRAILS OF '49

As part of the Trails of '49 celebration in 1930, a historic marker was dedicated to mark John Sutter's Hock Farm. *The Sutter County Farmer* of February 14, 1930, reported that over 20,000 people attended the celebration that also included a huge parade in Marysville.

The festivities started off in the morning with the dedication of a highway marker at Hock Farm, the old home of General John A. Sutter, and a long caravan of automobiles, old-time stage coaches drawn by horses and filled with men and women dressed in '49 costumes, mounted Indians, covered wagons and men and boys on horseback wended its way down the river road to the historic spot where General Sutter made his home for many years in the early days. There were two moving picture companies represented with their regular crews with cameras and microphones to "shoot" scenes and take the addresses during the ceremonies. The companies were the Paramount Picture Co. and the Pathe News Reel Co. There were over 1,000 in the assemblage. . . .Mrs. Annie Stuart Walters, a friend of General Sutter and a schoolmate of his grandchildren, was introduced as the guest of honor.

HAPPY BIRTHDAY, GEORGE

Yuba City Union High School directed a community effort on May 6, 1932, to produce a pageant honoring the 200th anniversary of the birth of George Washington. The patriotic drama encompassed all the prominent events of American history and involved a spectacular human flag. The event was held on the high school grounds, and *The Sutter County Farmer* reported that thousands watched "one of the greatest community events in the history of Sutter County."

YUBA CITY GOLDEN JUBILEE CELEBRATION

On the fiftieth anniversary of the incorporation of Yuba City in 1958, the local populace set about to mark the occasion with as much fun as possible while paying tribute to our hardy ancestors. A variety of events was set for the festive week in September. The Golden Jubilee Celebration kicked off with a street dance on Plumas Street. Joe Matthews Orchestra furnished the music, and many of the participants wore old-fashioned costumes and sported beards.

The Sutter County Historical Society depicted the typical home of fifty years ago in the old Purity Store on Plumas Street. About 25,000 people jammed the sidewalks of Plumas Street to watch the two-hour-long parade on Saturday afternoon. Captain Sacto, a television personality, was the parade grand marshal. Miss California, Sandra Lee Jennings of Riverside, attended the Saturday Jubilee events. She rode on the Pepsi-Cola float in the parade.

About 250 children participated in a kiddies' parade on Saturday morning. It was followed immediately by a hula-hoop contest with about 150 youngsters swiveling their hoops.

The Moose Lodge sponsored the rodeo both Saturday and Sunday, put on by Cotton Rosser of Marysville. It featured top clown acts and a "wild cow milking contest."

Mission Hall was built in 1909 by the Yuba City Ladies Improvement Club on Second Street across from the courthouse, where the county office building now stands. It has contained county offices and the library over the years. A penciled caption reads "Margaret & Thelma at Mission Hall–Yuba City."

The Yuba City Kiwanis Club members of 1930–1932 included many pillars of the community that worked together toward civic improvement.

The Yuba City Women's Clubhouse is on Plumas Street near the old City Hall, built in 1931 and pictured here in 1940.

The "Peach Girls" visit a peach orchard for a photo promoting the first Peach Day, June 3, 1922.

This replica of the mule-drawn streetcar was created for the Days of '49 celebration in 1930. The driver is Frank Ellis; Edward Von Geldern, who created the car for the parade, is on the back platform; and James Barr is standing at the window. Robert Morley has his chin on the window.

Meet the Prune family, mascots of the California Prune Festival that offered a weekend of music, food, and fun every September from 1988 through 2001 at the Yuba-Sutter Fairgrounds.

Gertrude Caldwell, Miss Yuba City, won second prize in the bathing beauty contest at the July 4, 1932 festivities at the Marysville Natatorium. Ernestine Graves of Oroville took first place, and Ruth Palm of Marysville was third.

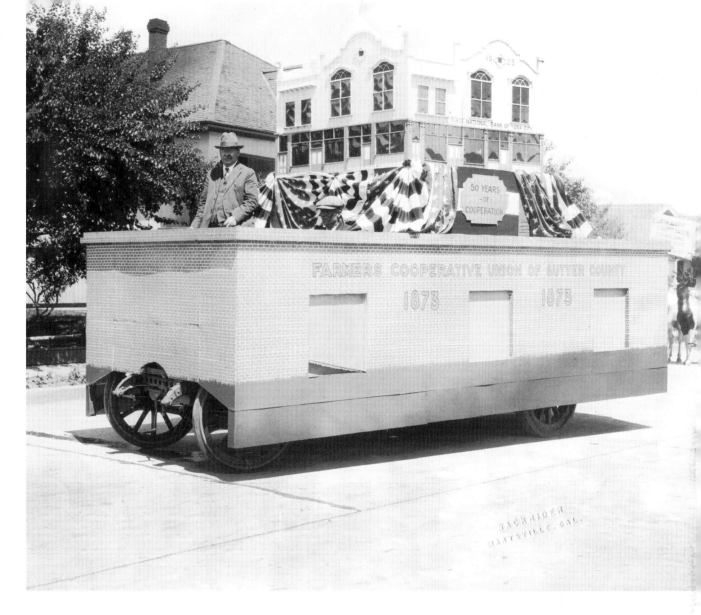

Sunday morning, a Car Gymkhana took place at the fairgrounds. There was a fly-in at the Sutter County Airport, which brought in forty-five people and one dog.

At the dance Saturday evening at the Yuba-Sutter Fairgrounds, Wayne Walkup won the title "King Whiskerino," and Mrs. Obie "Sandy" Wickersham was crowned Jubilee Queen by Miss California. Walter Galardi was honored for growing the least amount of beard since August 1st. Clarence A. Wessels bought the winning ticket for the big prize of a $3,000 lot. Music for the dance was by Ray Hackett's San Francisco Orchestra. The Golden Jubilee made Yuba City's fiftieth anniversary a week to remember.

A float designed by Edward Von Geldern for the Peach Day parade in August 1923 depicts the First National Bank of Yuba City and its growth from the Farmers Cooperative Union. C. R. Boyd, Sr., the bank president, rides on the float.

Yuba City
FUN AND GAMES

Yuba City has the good fortune to be situated in the center of a recreational paradise. The Feather River affords great opportunities for swimming, fishing, or boating.

Male swimmers enjoy the water park near the covered bridge, while females remain covered by voluminous clothing, circa 1900.

The Native Americans enjoyed the river too. Mrs. D. E. Bates, in her 1858 book, *Incidents on Land and Water or Four Years on the Pacific Coast*, described how the Maidu mothers placed their little ones in the shallow waters at the edge of the Feather River. "Their mothers learn them to swim, as soon as an old duck does her young. They build little pens at the brink of the river, so that the current cannot carry them down stream, put them in, and keep them there half the time. They really are amphibious."

From the time of earliest settlement, residents have found fun and refreshing relief from the valley's heat in the river. In the nineteenth century, swimmers dove or slid off a floating platform, or "resort," in the river.

Boathouses and docks have nearly always been present along the river. None have been permanent, as periodic high water tends to send them downstream. Many varieties of fish inhabit the river and are a welcome catch for the fishermen. The different seasons bring salmon, striped bass, shad, steelhead, trout, catfish, and sturgeon.

Boat racing has been an exciting and popular sport over the years. In the 1850s and 1860s, two steamships sometimes raced against each other coming up the Feather River, with a few well-placed bets on both sides. The passengers stood on deck, cheering on their boat, but it could be a dangerous sport if the boilers exploded. Several tragic accidents took place on the Feather River, with great loss of life.

In the 1930s, speedboat racing gained popularity. It was aided by the fact that Yuba City's Harold Rockholt built high-quality wooden speedboats made for racing. Rockholt boats set a standard for excellence, and vintage Rockholt boats are still highly valued today. Boat racing took place on the Feather River and, at times, on Ellis Lake. In the 1990s, jet boats from all over the world raced on the river.

"Navy Day Here Gives Thrills to Big Crowd: More Than 4,000 Enjoy Races of Fast Boats on the Feather River"
The Sutter County Farmer, May 20, 1932

Sunday was a big day in Yuba City. The Feather River Navy staged its first boat races before a crowd of more than 4,000 persons who came from far and near to enjoy the thrills of the fast racing craft.

Every race contained many thrills. There were two upsets and one spill and all of the speed and rivalry that goes to make a successful racing event.

So gratified were the members of the local club that they have started plans for another race here on July 4. . . . The race between Jack Wallace's River Rogue *and Ed von Geldern's* Argo *resulted in the* River Rogue *getting under the tape first but the* Argo *crew captured the ham suspended from the bridge when Bob Rush made a flying leap and swung on the ham as the boat went by. This stunt race was the cause of much merriment. . . .*

"Ten Persons in Danger as 'Argo' Founders in River"
The Sutter County Farmer, May 20, 1932

Ten well known local persons, including four women and a small child, had a thrilling experience Sunday evening when the Argo, *river boat of Edward von Geldern, foundered and almost sank in the Yuba river just above the junction of the Feather and Yuba.*

Damaged earlier in the day when it struck the east pier of the Feather river bridge while angling for position in the race against Jack

Wallace's River Rogue, *the boat sprung a leak while von Geldern and others on the boat with him were having chow mein at a Marysville restaurant.*

It appeared possible to control the water with the pumps and the boat started down the Yuba for the return to Yuba City. Passing under the Western Pacific bridge the boat grazed the pier sufficiently to open the leak.

Water poured in and stopped the engine, leaving the boat adrift in about 20 feet of water. Water climbed up onto the lower deck and passengers spent several anxious minutes as the boat floated downstream. By skillful maneuvering it was forced onto a sandbar on the Feather just below this city where the passengers waited in water knee deep until rescue arrived.

It was irony of fate that the River Rogue, *rival boat of the* Argo, *should be the rescue craft. Piloted by T. J. Rose, the boat went to the rescue and took off the passengers, thoroughly soaked but none the worse for their experience.*

The boat is still hanging onto the sandbar below town.

CELEBRITY AND THEATER

Yuba City girl Hazel Tharsing went on to become the noted stage actress Carlotta Monterey. Born in 1888, she won the Miss California title and embarked on a Broadway acting career. She met playwright Eugene O'Neill when she was chosen for a role in his play, *The Hairy Ape*. They were married in 1929, but O'Neill's addiction to alcohol and drugs dragged Carlotta in a downward spiral with him.

CRUISING

Many local "former teenagers" fondly recall cruising into Andy's Drive-In, Shan's on the southeast corner of Bridge and Plumas streets, or the Toot 'n Tell 'Em on Bridge Street, all favorites of the 1940s and 1950s. Drive-ins weren't a new idea, however. In 1929, an advertisement in the Yuba City High School *Highlights* read, "Drive in and Drink, Hot Lunches, Toasted Sandwiches, Tricolated Coffee, Tray Service to Your Car, Berg's."

Yuba City girl Hazel Tharsing went on to become the noted stage actress Carlotta Monterey.

Motorboats race past avid fans on the Feather River in the 1930s.

Swimmers prepare to slide into the Feather River in 1897 or 1898.

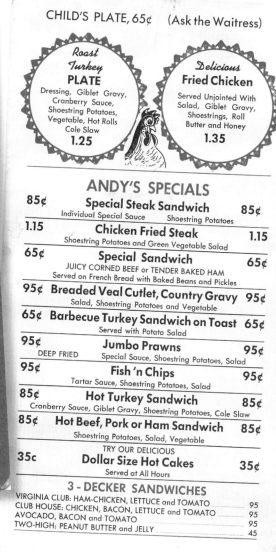

Roast Turkey PLATE
Dressing, Giblet Gravy, Cranberry Sauce, Shoestring Potatoes, Vegetable, Hot Rolls Cole Slaw
1.25

Delicious **Fried Chicken**
Served Unjointed With Salad, Giblet Gravy, Shoestrings, Roll Butter and Honey
1.35

ANDY'S SPECIALS

85¢	**Special Steak Sandwich**	85¢
	Individual Special Sauce Shoestring Potatoes	
1.15	**Chicken Fried Steak**	1.15
	Shoestring Potatoes and Green Vegetable Salad	
65¢	**Special Sandwich**	65¢
	JUICY CORNED BEEF or TENDER BAKED HAM	
	Served on French Bread with Baked Beans and Pickles	
95¢	**Breaded Veal Cutlet, Country Gravy**	95¢
	Salad, Shoestring Potatoes and Vegetable	
65¢	**Barbecue Turkey Sandwich on Toast**	65¢
	Served with Potato Salad	
95¢	**Jumbo Prawns**	95¢
	DEEP FRIED Special Sauce, Shoestring Potatoes, Salad	
95¢	**Fish 'n Chips**	95¢
	Tartar Sauce, Shoestring Potatoes, Salad	
85¢	**Hot Turkey Sandwich**	85¢
	Cranberry Sauce, Giblet Gravy, Shoestring Potatoes, Cole Slaw	
85¢	**Hot Beef, Pork or Ham Sandwich**	85¢
	Shoestring Potatoes, Salad, Vegetable	
35c	TRY OUR DELICIOUS **Dollar Size Hot Cakes**	35¢
	Served at All Hours	

3 - DECKER SANDWICHES

VIRGINIA CLUB: HAM-CHICKEN, LETTUCE and TOMATO	95
CLUB HOUSE: CHICKEN, BACON, LETTUCE and TOMATO	95
AVOCADO, BACON and TOMATO	95
TWO-HIGH: PEANUT BUTTER and JELLY	45

Andy's Drive-In was a popular teenage hangout opened by Andy Swenson in 1947 on the northwest corner of Plumas Street and Colusa Highway. There were booths and a counter inside, but the action was outside, where carhops in blue and white uniforms took orders and delivered food on trays that hooked onto car windows.

Foxhunters pose for a photo with their prey in the 1890s. Elmer Jackson is third from left in the back row.

The covered bridge on the Feather River towered over the boat dock, circa 1900.

The Yuba City swimming pool was built along the edge of the Feather River in 1941.

Fishermen display an impressive sturgeon from the Feather River in 1910.

Swimmers enjoy the Feather River near the railroad bridge in the 1920s.

The Hub City Merchants played independent baseball in the Westside Park that Fred Cooper built near his dairy on Bridge Street, circa 1908–1909. Front row: Elmer "Brick" Booth, Harvey Spillman, Jack Wallace, and Louis Harris. Back row: George Sanders, Frank Booth, Sr., Russell Kane, William Spillman (manager), Jimmy Russell, and Clarence Hopkins.

YubA City —5   9-25-47
        vs
MAR Ysville —1

First opening of Park Under lights

The Yuba City Bears beat the Marysville team at Bryant Park, Marysville, in the first game under lights, on September 25, 1947.

Yuba and Sutter
SPORTSMEN'S CLUB

First
Annual
SHAD BAKE
Feather River
June 16, '12

The Yuba and Sutter Sportsmen's Club members disport themselves at the First Annual Shad Bake at the Feather River on June 16, 1912. The committee prepared and cooked the fish on wooden boards propped next to the fire. Meanwhile, the most popular spot was the improvised bar. Finally, the succulent shad was ready and served with plenty of beer. After eating, they relaxed with cigars and good-natured fellowship.

Yuba City
OUR TOWN

Yuba City's business district began on Second Street and then flowed up Bridge Street before expanding down Plumas Street.

YUBA CITY'S SISTER CITY

The Yuba City Sister City Association was formed in 1989, when Yuba City agreed to become a Sister City to Fujishiro, Japan. Fujishiro and Yuba City are quite similar in that they both have a small mountain range nearby (the Sutter Buttes and Mt. Tskuba); each have two rivers in the area (Feather and Yuba rivers near Yuba City and Tone and Kokai rivers near Fujishiro); each are near a major city (Sacramento and Tokyo); and their main crop is rice.

The primary purpose of the exchange is education for the students. Each year, about fifteen Yuba City students visit Fujishiro in May, and the Japanese students visit Yuba City in October. Adults also travel back and forth, and both they and the students stay in local homes to learn about the culture.

This view of Bridge Street, looking west from the grade to the covered bridge, was taken by Clara Smith around 1900. The mule-drawn trolley is approaching the bridge, and the tracks are visible in the foreground. The building at the corner of Bridge and Second streets housed C. S. Duncan's grocery.

When the larger neighboring city of Toride (tore-ih-day) annexed Fujishiro about three years ago, Toride then became Yuba City's Sister City. Yearly visits continue between the two sister cities, and the participants form lasting friendships. In 2009, the sister cities will celebrate twenty years of exchanges, learning, and friendships across the world.

Butchers and patrons pause inside the People's Meat Market on Second Street between Fairman and Bridge streets circa 1910. Note the sausages hanging at left.

Edward Duplex, who later became the mayor of Wheatland and the first black mayor west of the Mississippi, established a hair dressing and shaving saloon in the Schuessler's Building on Bridge Street in Yuba City. After about a year, he relocated to Wheatland.

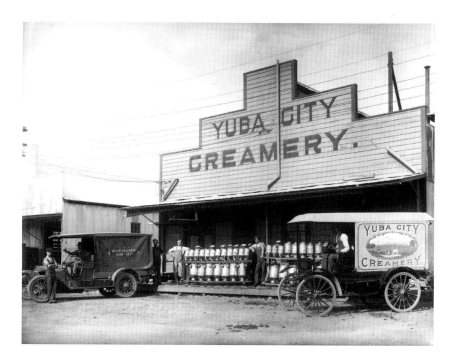

George Gallatin and crew display the Yuba City Creamery delivery trucks. Gallatin opened the creamery in 1910 on Sutter Street and owned an adjoining bakery on Second Street. The creamery boasted a 600-pound churn.

The First National Bank building on Bridge Street later housed other banks and offices.

yuba City.
Lower Bridge St.

This view of Bridge Street looking west from Second Street shows yet unpaved streets and the horse trough in front of the grocery store.

Second Street, 1920s

Highway 99 passed along Bridge Street in the 1940s. Ahead in the distance are the bridge and Veterans' Park.

A view looking north on Plumas Street in the 1930s reveals a busy town center.

P. W. Griffiths took this view from atop the Hall of Records around 1900. On B Street, the residences of McQuaid and H. Moncur are on the south side. On the north side of B Street are the homes of A. H. Hewitt on the east, and proceeding west, Dr. Lyman, W. F. Peck, and Peters. In the distance are the M. E. Church and Yuba City Cemetery. Dr. Teegarden's house is visible on the city border.

THE HOME OF THE TRAVELING MAN FOR SOLID COMFORT.

PHONE 160   YUBA CITY, CAL.

5 CTS. CAR FARE FROM MARYSVILLE.

HOTEL SUTTER

EUROPEAN PLAN

MRS. A. M. DAVIS, PROP.

FIRST-CLASS DINING AND BAR SERVICE AT POPULAR PRICES

ALL OUTSIDE ROOMS. STRICTLY MODERN.
ROOMS $1.00 DAY UP. WITH BATH $1.50 UP.
SPECIAL RATES TO PERMANENT GUESTS.

Hotel Sutter
Yuba City, Cal.

Informal Opening Banquet
Wednesday Evening, May 3, 1911

The Hotel Sutter on Bridge Street opened on the corner of Bridge and Sutter streets on May 3, 1911.

Program

Gern's Orchestra

1. MARCH - - "Under the Banner of Victory"

2. SELECTION - - From the "Chocolate Soldier"

3. OVERTURE - "The Time, the Place and the Girl"

4. "GLOW WORM" Ideal - - P. Linke

5. GRAND SELECTION - - "Lucrezia Borgia"

6. CELLO SOLO - - (a) "Simple Aveu"
   (b) "Traumerei"

7. SELECTION - From "The Merry Widow"

8. SELECTION - - - From "Woodland"

9. SELECTION - - From "Madame Sherry"
   "Every Little Movement Has a Meaning All Its Own"

10. SELECTIONS - - - - By Request

Menu

Martini Cocktail

Oyster Cocktail
Salted Almonds   California Ripe Olives
Sweet Pickles

Baked Barracuda
Madiera Sauce   Parisienne Potatoes

Cala-Zinfandel
Calif. Winery
Sacto., Cal.

Filet of Beef
a la Petits Pois

Roman Punch

Roast Chicken   Giblet Sauce
French Fried Potatoes
Cold Asparagus   Mayonnaise

Salad Macedoine

Champagne
Paul Mason

Neapolitan Ice Cream
Assorted Cake

Fruits   Nuts   Raisins

Camenbert Cheese
Bent Crackers

Cigars

Coffee

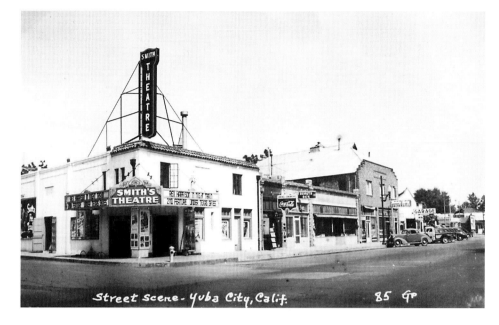

Street Scene - Yuba City, Calif. 85 GP

Smith's Theatre at the corner of Plumas Street and Forbes Avenue showed the double feature *Night Train* with Rex Harrison and *Under Texas Skies*, both released in 1940.

Plumas Street, 1940

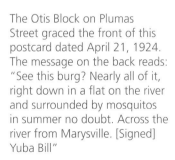

The Otis Block on Plumas Street graced the front of this postcard dated April 21, 1924. The message on the back reads: "See this burg? Nearly all of it, right down in a flat on the river and surrounded by mosquitos in summer no doubt. Across the river from Marysville. [Signed] Yuba Bill"

Otis Block, Plumas Street   Yuba City California

Vehicles coming off the Twin Cities Bridge into Yuba City pass the Subway Garage and Yuba City Fruit Market, as eastbound cars head to Marysville in the 1930s.

You Are Invited...

HONORABLE RORY RAMIREZ

YUBA CITY'S CENTENNIAL MAYOR

SWEARING-IN CEREMONY & CELEBRATION

The celebration of the one hundredth anniversary of Yuba City's incorporation began with the swearing in of Mayor Rory Ramirez.

The Associated gas station epitomized Art Moderne architecture in Yuba City in 1940.

A major Plumas Street improvement and beautification project is underway, to be completed in 2009.

Yuba City Hall is an innovative, modern building, designed by Foothill Designs Group in the early 1980s. It features a low profile surrounded by insulating berms and situated for solar efficiency. Its tranquil beauty is an inspiring departure point for quality city government.

As Plumas Street opens in a wide boulevard to the south of Bridge Street, the new town center features a splendid fountain along the pleasant street where new medical buildings line either side.

Yuba City
HOME SWEET HOME

We have some examples of fine homes built by proud residents of Yuba City.

The Phipps House at 246 B Street was built around 1881. It was an early hotel and boardinghouse, and it continues in use today as apartments.

The Grant family gathers in front of their Yuba City residence. Mrs. Grant, with a parasol, is on the veranda. Jim on the porch, and Alex is at the gate. Graeme, Mary, Constance, and Jessie stand in front of the picket fence.

Wheat farmer Frederic Dahling hired Swain & Hudson to build his 4,000-square-foot Italianate villa at 2600 Lincoln Road. Completed in 1886, it was so large that it was used as a landmark in northern California surveys. In 1917, Dahling switched to growing peaches and was known for his "Dahling Home" brand.

The Italianate Victorian at 422 Second Street was built around 1880. Owned by Idalean McCampbell, it may have been the first house in Yuba City to be equipped with electricity in the 1890s.

Around 1900, the Teegarden-Mosburg House at 731 Plumas Street was a ranch house on a country lane, which became Teegarden Avenue. Built in the 1880s for Dr. Eli Teegarden, it has had a varied history as family home, mortuary, and rooming house.

The Jacob Onstott family gathers in front of their 1880s Italianate-style home at 2078 Colusa Highway. Jake and his brother J. P. Onstott grew Thompson Seedless grapes and owned dry yards. They founded the raisin industry, shipping raisins to the East Coast. This brick tank house was one of two existing in California when it was razed by a developer. The house itself was bulldozed one night in 2003, and Yuba City lost the distinctive landmark on its western border.

The James T. Bogue house was built of redwood in the late 1880s. Note the tank house and windmill on the right. Bogue owned a large nursery, orchards, and a vineyard. The entire area surrounding his ranch was called the Bogue District.

The S. G. Deaner family shows off their home on Second Street in Yuba City in June 1892. Deaner was the sheriff in Yuba City in 1882–1884.

The largest known walnut tree in the world grew in the yard of the Dr. Lyman home at 229 B Street. It was measured in 1915 at about forty-five years of age when it was over 100 feet in height and had a spread of 111 feet. Its girth was twenty-five feet around. It was taken down in 1940.

The Dr. Barr home at 365 Second Street is an example of Prairie-style architecture with a Craftsman influence, built in the early 1920s. Dr. Barr was an area physician and very active in social and civic affairs.

PRESERVATION

These historic buildings have each found an adaptive re-use. Their current owners are preserving them as they meet today's needs, all the while reminding us of Yuba City's heritage.

The Harkey House at 212 C Street bears the name of William Harkey, elected Sutter County Sheriff in 1873. Wanting to live close to the courthouse, he built this handsome home in 1874. Now, as Harkey House Bed & Breakfast, it continues to delight guests at well over a century and a quarter.

The Crowhurst family grew up in this Victorian-era house at 661 Shasta Street. The house has found an adaptive reuse as an heirloom nursery in Vintagehouse Nursery.

The Littlejohn House, built in 1899, is owned by the City of Yuba City and now houses the Yuba City Parks and Recreation Department. This house is a success story for historic preservation in Yuba City. With a commercial partner, the precursor to the neighboring Winco store, the city facilitated the renovation and preservation of this significant historic resource. The Littlejohn House continues to serve as a unique landmark that demarcates the southern approach to Yuba City.

A crowd braves the rain to observe the one hundredth birthday of the Hall of Records, complete with birthday cake. In 1991, the building still functioned as the county clerk and recorder's office. It subsequently moved across the street to larger quarters, and the Hall of Records found new use as chambers for the Board of Supervisors.

Yuba City
PRESERVING OUR PAST

The William L. Conkey Rose Garden is in Howard Harter Park behind the Community Memorial Museum.

Twenty-one local citizens interested in the history of our area came together in 1954 to form the Sutter County Historical Society. The group's purpose was "to collect and preserve" records and artifacts of Sutter County. Their goal was to create a museum.

The first museum was in a storefront in the new Carriage Square shopping center that opened May 1964. In October, the Sutter County Supervisors took over the museum as a county facility, with the agreement that the Historical Society would continue to operate it. Mrs. Ida Doty served as the chair of the Museum Committee for ten years. Historical Society members volunteered in many capacities to keep the museum open.

In 1972, Howard and Norma Harter donated about six acres on Butte House Road for a memorial park. The following year, they made a gift of $100,000 to establish a trust fund for a museum building on the property. Then Gilbert Williamson and Mr. and Mrs. Wilfred Williams donated funds to purchase additional property needed for the building site. Many, many donations were given by the community to fund the building costs. The Sutter County Board of Supervisors accepted the gift of the park and building and agreed to administer and maintain the museum and grounds. The Harters personally oversaw the planting of more than 300 trees in the park.

The building was completed by April 1975. With hard work by Historical Society volunteers and the first curator Jean Gustin, artifacts were transferred from the Carriage Square museum and arranged in the new facility. Help also came from members of the new Museum Auxiliary, and the Community Memorial Museum was dedicated on October 19, 1975, to a warm reception from the community. The mission of the museum is to collect, preserve, and interpret the history of Sutter County. Financial and volunteer support from the community over the years has been key to the continued growth and vitality of the museum.

The Howard Harter Park has been developed in recent years into a beautiful, passive-use park with walking paths, a butterfly garden, and a formal rose garden. It has come a long way from the beginning when "the volunteer barley crop was harvested, netting $160.87" for the park. Now the Sutter Buttes Garden Club grooms and maintains the memorial rose garden, making it a lovely setting for weddings and events, and the park is enjoyed by visitors every day.

The Community Memorial Museum of Sutter County at 1333 Butte House Road was built in 1975. Open Tuesday through Sunday, admission is free. Changing exhibits, programs for adults and children, a museum store, and continued expansion keep the museum fresh and intriguing for visitors.

APPENDIX

An unsettled period in city politics occurred in the late 1940s and 1950s, perhaps as a result of growing pains of the town. On June 20, 1949, the City Council meeting was particularly turbulent. In a period of less than an hour, Yuba City had three different mayors. Howard Harter was voted out of office by fellow council members. Former mayor Perry Mosburg was named mayor, but he declined a few moments later. The game of musical mayors ended up with Lloyd Huse in charge.

In 1954, citizens instituted a recall of two councilmen. Raymond Butler lost his seat in a special election, but J. W. Sanderson retained his by a narrow margin. In a second special election in 1954, Annabelle Martin won the empty council seat by only eleven votes to become the first woman to serve on the Yuba City Council.

Following the 1955 flood, the Sutter County Grand Jury, responding to citizens' concerns, launched an investigation into the handling of city and county affairs during the flood. As a result, eleven officials were rebuked by the Grand Jury for their mishandled affairs. Mayor Glenn Gauche resigned, followed by Councilman N. Paul Hansen.

YUBA CITY MAYORS

January 27, 1908	J. W. Ashley
April 1910—April 1914	Richard Walton
April 1918	E. J. White
May 1924	Hugh D. Moncur
April 1926—April 1930	Richard Walton
April 1930	Claude Triplett
April 1932	J. H. LePine
April 1934—April 1940	Edward D. Benham
April 1940—April 1942	Arthur H. Scott
April 1942—April 1944	Ed Wilson
April 1946—April 1947	H. D. "John" Huse
April 1947—May 1949	Perry Mosburg
June 1949—April 1951	Lloyd I. Huse
April 1951—April 1952	Riley W. Young
April 1952—April 1953	Howard Harter
April 1953—April 1954	J. W. Sanderson
April 1954—October 1954	Raymond T. Butler
October 1954—April 1956	Glenn Gauche
April 1956—April 1957	James F. Henderson
April 1957—April 1958	Lawrence Mark
April 1958—April 1959	James J. Oakham
April 1959—April 1960	Dale A. Tressler
April 1960—April 1961	Joseph D. Fraser
April 1961—October 1961	John E. Litwin
April 1962—September 1962	Al Rose
October 1962—April 1963	Richard Rhodes

April 1963—April 1964	Kenneth H. Hopper
April 1964—April 1965	Ray Tiner
April 1965—April 1966	Marion E. Underhill
April 1966—April 1967	Henry Lamon
April 1967—August 1967	Lonny L. Renfrow
August 1967—April 1968	Lawrence Mark
April 1968—April 1969	Richard Young
April 1969—April 1970	R. Hoberg
April 1970—April 1971	Joseph D. Fraser
April 1971—April 1972	Lawrence Mark
April 1972—April 1973	Robert Caplan
April 1973—April 1974	Henry Lamon
April 1974—April 1975	Joseph D. Fraser
April 1975—April 1976	Lawrence Mark
April 1976—April 1977	Tom Pfeffer
April 1977—April 1978	Joe Benatar
April 1978—April 1979	Joseph D. Fraser
April 1979—April 1980	Lawrence Mark
April 1980—April 1981	Charles Pappageorge
April 1981—April 1982	Tom Pfeffer
April 1982—December 1982	Ronald Southard
December 1982—December 1983	Lawrence Mark
December 1983—December 1984	Joseph D. Fraser
December 1984—November 1985	Charles Pappageorge
November 1985—December 1986	Ronald Southard
December 1986—November 1987	George Garcia
November 1987—December 1988	Lawrence Mark
December 1988—November 1989	William Meagher
November 1989—November 1990	Dennis Nelson
November 1990—November 1991	Charles Pappageorge
November 1991—November 1992	Bob Barkhouse
November 1992—November 1993	Karen Cartoscelli
November 1993—November 1994	Dennis Nelson
November 1994—November 1995	Sandra M. Hilliard
November 1995—November 1996	Pat Hearne
November 1996—November 1997	Karen Cartoscelli
November 1997—November 1998	Lee Welch
November 1998—November 1999	Bob Barkhouse
November 1999—November 2000	Sandra M. Hilliard
November 2000—November 2001	David Doolittle
November 2001—November 2002	Lee Welch
November 2002—November 2003	Bob Barkhouse
November 2003—November 2004	Sandra M. Hilliard
November 2004—November 2005	Karen Cartoscelli
November 2005—November 2006	Eric Hellberg
November 2006—November 2007	John Miller
November 2007	Rory Ramirez

CITY STREETS

Here are some of Yuba City's familiar streets and how they were named.

A through G Streets, and First through Fourth Streets—Joseph S. Ruth was hired by the town's founders to survey and lay out Yuba City. He used a grid pattern, with A Street running perpendicular to Second Street. Today, only a remnant of A Street exists, along with B, C, and Second streets.

Bogue Road—was named for nurseryman and orchardist James Bogue. The old Bogue home is on Bogue Road between Garden Highway and Railroad Avenue. Where it once stood surrounded by orchards, it is now in the middle of a housing development. Half a mile to the west was Bogue Station, a stop on the railroad line where fruit was loaded to be shipped out.

Bremer Avenue—Christian Bremer arrived in the early 1870s, and his nephew August Bremer came in 1878. His son, Frank G. Bremer, founded Bremer's Hardware, a longtime business on Second Street (1907–2007).

Butte House Road—was originally an Indian trail. It was the site of the "Butte House," a hotel and stage stop built in 1855, near the present town of Sutter, along the old wagon road.

Cooper Avenue and Frederick Street—were named for the Frederick Cooper family. They had a large acreage of orchards and a dry yard and packinghouse for processing their fruit. Their family home still stands on the northwest corner of Cooper and B streets. In the 1920s, they opened the Cooper Tract for development, and many homes were built there.

Harter Road—was named for George Harter, a native of Ohio. When he arrived in California in 1866, he began cutting wood. He went into the freighting business, hauling supplies to the mines and hauling back loads of timber which he used to build his two-story house and barns in 1871–1872. He eventually acquired 800 acres of land, on which he grew grain. His sons planted orchards, established a dry yard to dry the fruit, and founded the Harter Cannery. It was a flourishing business that employed many locals during the summer harvest. It is closed now, and the sturdy pioneer Harter home, overrun by development, was slated for demolition when it burned several years ago.

Honor Oak Lane—is a combination of Howard and Norma Harter's first names. At 1515 Honor Oak Lane, the old Samuel Stabler home, was an ancient oak tree called the Honor Oak. A souvenir piece of the tree, salvaged when the tree had to be taken down, may be seen at the Community Memorial Museum.

Hunn Road—was named for Edwin A. Hunn, who was the leading brick contractor in the area. At age sixteen, he learned the brick trade in San Francisco after the 1906 earthquake. He came to Sutter County in 1919 and bought ten acres on Franklin Road to plant to peaches. He worked as a brick mason and founded the Marysville Brick Company.

Kiley Avenue—David and Julia Kiley purchased the Teegarden house on Plumas Street in 1904. In 1906, the area was resurveyed, and the street was likely named Kiley at that time.

Littlejohn Road—was named for James Littlejohn, an Ohio native. He followed the overland trail and arrived in California at age twenty-four. He eventually purchased 500 acres, including some of the James Gray homestead, and built a house and barns. He raised racehorses and was instrumental in establishing the Yuba City Grange. The house burned in 1899, and the Littlejohns built a new home at the corner of Franklin Road and Highway 99 that is still standing.

McRae Way—was named after A. S. McRae, who owned the McRae grocery store in the 1860s.

Ohleyer Road—was named for George Ohleyer, who arrived in 1852 from the Alsace-Lorraine region of France. He acquired and farmed 960 acres of valley farmland. In 1882, Ohleyer, with several partners, bought the *Sutter Banner* and the *Yuba City Journal* newspapers, consolidating them into *The Sutter County Farmer*. As editor, he used the newspaper as a voice for the Anti-Debris Movement and helped in the farmers' fight against hydraulic mining and the ruin it brought to fertile farmlands in the valley.

Percy Avenue—was named for A. J. Percy, who crossed the plains to California in 1849. Originally from Maine, he prospected and drove teams to the mines. He then went into the livery business in Marysville before buying a 126-acre ranch near Yuba City.

Rosalind Avenue—was named after Rosalind Schneider of the Schneider clothing and shoe store. Their home was west of Cooper, almost to Clark Avenue.

Stabler Lane—was named for Samuel Stabler, who was the county clerk and recorder as well as district attorney for two terms, after which he established the law offices of Stabler and Bayne in Yuba City and Colusa. When he retired, he bought a 208-acre ranch west of Yuba City in 1886, where he raised Thompson Seedless Grapes. He built a family home, warehouses, and a dry yard in 1892. Eventually, his son Harry Stabler took over management of the ranch. On Harry's death, his sister sold the property to Howard and Norma Harter. They later developed the land into the Honor Oak subdivision. The Stabler home remains a timeless landmark on nearby Honor Oak Lane.

Teegarden Avenue—was named after prominent physician Dr. Eli Teegarden, who built the Teegarden house at 731 Plumas Street about 1880.

Tharp Road—was named for Robert W. Tharp, a native of Missouri, who came to California in 1869 at age thirty-one. He became a Sutter County farmer, and his son Charles was among the first to have peach orchards in the Tierra Buena area.

Walton Avenue—was named for B. F. and O. M. Walton, brothers who arrived in Yuba City in 1859. They were prominent farmers, and Benjamin Franklin Walton was instrumental in establishing the Farmers' Cooperative Union. Their descendant, Richard Walton, was elected to the City Council in 1910 and served a term as mayor.

Whyler Road—was named after William Whyler, who arrived in Sutter County in 1852 after mining in the mountains.

City Parks

A few of Yuba City's parks were named for historical figures.

Blackburn-Talley Sports Complex/Park—was named after three men who died while trying to warn residents to evacuate in the 1955 flood. They were overtaken by water from the break at Shanghai Bend. Sutter County Undersheriff Charles Earl Blackburn and his son, Robert W. Blackburn, and Deputy Sheriff John Leroy Talley all gave their lives to help the citizens of Yuba City.

Gauche Park—home of the new state-of-the-art aquatic park, was named for the former mayor Glenn Gauche, who served during the 1955 flood.

Sam Brannan Park—was named for one of the founders of Yuba City, a Mormon pioneer, who spread the word through the streets of San Francisco about the discovery of gold at Coloma. He is credited with sparking the gold fever that spread worldwide. His business investments and speculations boosted his fortune with a meteoric rise, and then fell just as rapidly into poverty.

SELECTED BIBLIOGRAPHY

Anderson, Walt. *Inland Island: The Sutter Buttes*. Prescott, Arizona and Live Oak, California: Natural Selection and the Middle Mountain Foundation, 2004.

Chamberlain, William H., and Harry L. Wells. *History of Sutter County California with Illustrations*. Oakland, California: Thompson & West, 1879.

Chartkoff, Joseph L., and Kerry Kona Chartkoff. *The Archaeology of California*. Stanford, California: Stanford University Press, 1984.

Delay, Peter J. *History of Yuba and Sutter Counties, California, with Biographical Sketches*. Los Angeles, California: Historic Record Company, 1924.

Guinn, J. M. *History of the State of California and Biographic Record of the Sacramento Valley, California*. Chicago, Illinois: The Chapman Publishing Co., 1906.

Hanson, William P. Diaries of William Hanson, including recollections of Honorable D. M. Hanson crossing the plains in 1849, written in 1919. Meriam Library, California State University, Chico.

Heizer, Robert F., ed. *Handbook of North American Indians*. Vol. 8. Washington, D.C.: Smithsonian Institution, 1978.

Hurtado, Albert L. *Indian Survival on the California Frontier*. Yale University Press: 1988.

Lowe, Jacqueline, Julie Stark, and Danae McDougal-Stewart. *Worth Keeping: An Architectural History of Sutter and Yuba Counties, California*. Yuba City, California: Community Memorial Museum of Sutter County. Marysville, California: Mary Aaron Memorial Museum, 1990.

Lowe, Jacqueline, Sharyl Simmons, and Julie Stark, eds. *Coping With Disaster: Voices From the 1955 Flood*. Yuba City, California: Community Memorial Museum of Sutter County, 1995.

Memorial and Biographical History of Northern California, Illustrated. Chicago, Illinois: The Lewis Publishing Company, 1891.

Shoenherr, Allan A. *A Natural History of California*. Berkeley, California: University of California Press, 1992.

Vale, Thomas R., ed. *Fire, Native Peoples, and the Natural Landscape*. Washington, D.C.: Island Press, 2002.

NEWSPAPERS

Appeal-Democrat
Daily Appeal
Independent-Farmer
Independent Herald
Marysville Appeal
Sutter County Banner
Sutter County Farmer

INDEX

Photo courtesy Ken Calhoun

When you see the Buttes, you know you're home.